Disciples

Year 2

overcoming sin

Rebecca Konyndyk DeYoung

FAITH
ALIVE®
Christian Resources

Grand Rapids, Michigan

Mixed Sources

Product group from well-managed
forests and other controlled sources
www.fsc.org Cert no. SW-COC-002283
© 1996 Forest Stewardship Council

Photos: iStockphoto

This study is part of *Disciples,* year 2, a comprehensive multiyear faith formation program for adults. Year 2 studies build on the foundation laid by the studies in year 1.

Year 2 includes the following study guides, which feature daily readings for each session.

- Prayer
- Reading the Bible
- Worship
- Living in Community
- Overcoming Sin

Unless otherwise indicated, Scripture quotations in this publication are from the Holy Bible, Today's New International Version, © 2001, 2005 by the International Bible Society. All rights reserved worldwide. Used by permission.

We welcome your comments. Call us at 1-800-333-8300 or e-mail us at editors@faithaliveresources.org.

ISBN 978-1-59255-436-2

10 9 8 7 6 5 4 3 2 1

Contents

Introduction 5

Session 1: The Roots and Branches of Sin 8
   1. Looking Forward 10
   2. A Substitute for Happiness. 14
   3. Pride: The Queen of the Vices 18
   4. Vainglory: Appearance, Attention, Approval 22
   5. Relying on God's Power 26
   Discussion Guide. 31

Session 2: Envy 38
   1. Winners and Losers 40
   2. Poison Fruit 44
   3. The Enemy of Love. 48
   4. Haves and Have-nots 52
   5. Apprentices 56
   Discussion Guide. 61

Session 3: Wrath 66
   1. Emotion or Sin? 68
   2. Holy Anger. 72
   3. Out of Control 76
   4. Selfless or Selfish? 80
   5. Slow to Anger 84
   Discussion Guide. 87

Session 4: Gluttony 94
    1. A Selfish Obsession 96
    2. F.R.E.S.H. 100
    3. Sneaky Snacking 104
    4. Meal Ready to Eat 108
    5. Fasting 112
    Discussion Guide 117

Session 5: Sloth 122
    1. The Noonday Demon 124
    2. The Demands of Love 128
    3. Too Busy? 132
    4. A Change of Heart 136
    5. Perseverance 140
    Discussion Guide 145

Session 6: Greed 152
    1. The Freedom of Generosity 154
    2. Mine! 158
    3. No Fear 162
    4. The Love of Money 166
    5. Simplicity 170
    Discussion Guide 175

Session 7: Lust 180
    1. Mixed Messages 182
    2. Love versus Lust 186
    3. Collateral Damage 190
    4. Sticky Tape 194
    5. Chastity 198
    Discussion Guide 203

Introduction

Most Christians today have forgotten about the seven deadly sins. Either that or they misunderstand them. Perhaps that is because the list is old—dating back to the earliest centuries of the Christian church. It was originally designed to examine the impact of sin on our discipleship, to give us a roadmap for self-examination and a plan for spiritual development.

Our aim in this book is to walk contemporary disciples though this ancient pattern of growth in godliness. We are convinced that what Christian saints and sages of the past have to say about the different ways sin can entangle us is as relevant today as the day they wrote it. Together we'll look at each of those sins in order to become better disciples of Jesus Christ.

Be Transformed!

We don't often use the language of virtues and vices anymore. But many early Christians used it to describe the process the apostle Paul talks about in his letter to the Colossians:

> Put to death, therefore, whatever belongs to your earthly nature. . . . You used to walk in these ways, in the life you once lived. But now you must also rid yourselves of all such things . . . since you have taken off your old self with its practices and have put on the new self, which is being renewed in knowledge in the image of its Creator (Col. 3:5, 7-10).

Faith is supposed to change us, Paul tells the Christian believers. To believe is to follow the way of Christ. And to follow means taking off our old, sinful nature, with its habits of thought and behavior, and becoming someone new. Put on your new identity in Christ, Paul says, with its renewed and godly habits of thought and behavior. Let the Spirit transform you.

Christian thinkers in the early church and throughout the Middle Ages thought of "taking off the sinful nature" and "putting on Christ" as a transformation of character (Rom. 12:2). They described the sinful nature in terms of vices, and the sanctified nature in terms of virtues like those listed in Colossians 3:12, 14: "Clothe yourselves with compassion, kindness, humility, gentleness and patience. . . . And over all these virtues put on love, which binds them all together in perfect unity." The transformation from a sinful to a Christlike character is the heart of spiritual formation.

The Task of a Lifetime

This study will take us on a spiritual journey into a deeper relationship with Jesus Christ. Our walk with him is an attempt to imitate his actions—but even more, to become the kind of person he is. The journey depends on the relationship. The vices are not merely another set of "thou shalt nots" to avoid with self-satisfied, legalistic hearts. Nor can we purge our lives of evil practices by our own effort—for that we need the grace given by the Holy Spirit to work in our hearts. But receiving grace is not a passive thing! It gives us a call to action, a gift to use, and a relationship to cultivate. We show our confidence in God's grace when we seek to grow and keep growing spiritually.

A Curriculum on Spiritual Formation

Our purpose is not to wallow in the inevitability of sin or feel guilty about it. Rather, "[Christ's] divine power has given us everything we need for a godly life" (2 Pet. 1:3). In Christ, by the power of the Holy Spirit, we are *overcomers*. Our lives and character are being transformed to become more like Jesus.

So our objective is to help disciples of Jesus today embark on the same lifelong journey of spiritual progress and practice as Christians before them. In this study, we will translate centuries of spiritual wisdom and advice into language and life lessons that contemporary Christ-followers can understand and apply to themselves.

Each session offers

- five daily readings for each small group discussion, with questions to ponder and suggestions for action.
- a small group discussion guide.

And there's more. At our website, www.GrowDisciples.org, you'll find links for anyone who wants to dig deeper into each one of these sins and the opposing virtues.

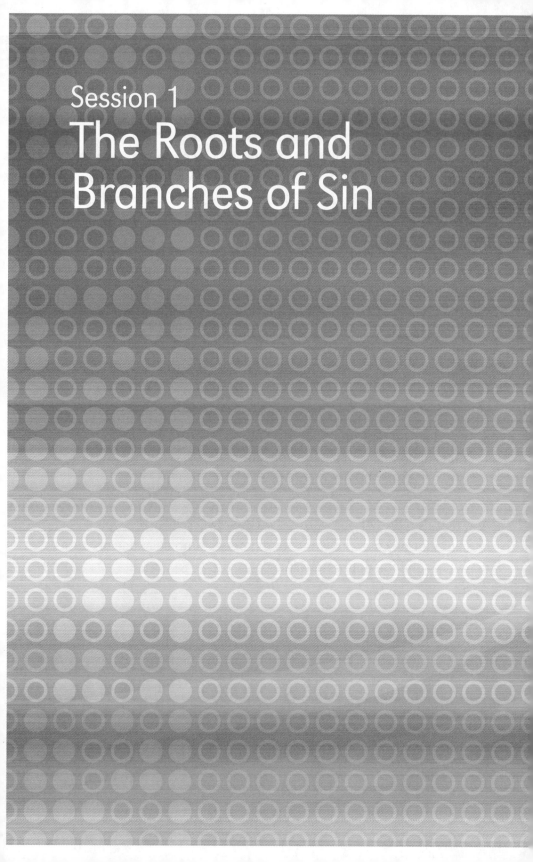

Session 1
The Roots and Branches of Sin

Looking Forward 1

"Do not lie to each other, since you have taken off your old self with its practices and have put on the new self, which is being renewed in knowledge in the image of its Creator. Here there is no Gentile or Jew, circumcised or uncircumcised, barbarian, Scythian, slave or free, but Christ is all, and is in all. Therefore, as God's chosen people, holy and dearly loved, clothe yourselves with compassion, kindness, humility, gentleness and patience. Bear with each other and forgive one another if any of you has a grievance against someone. Forgive as the Lord forgave you. And over all these virtues put on love, which binds them all together in perfect unity."

—Colossians 3:9-14

Imagine that you were going to die tomorrow. What speech would your family and friends give at your funeral? How would they sum up who you were and what your life was like? Eulogies at funerals are probably the closest thing we have nowadays to the examination of our character and our life as a whole. What might such a reflection teach you about yourself and the shape of your life?

Now imagine something else. What if you were to write that speech now, *before* you die, as a picture of the sort of person you would like to become—and then spent the rest of your life trying to live up to it? Looking forward, instead of backward, we get a sense of what regular self-examination and spiritual disciplines are for. They are for helping us become re-formed people. Actually, the work of writing down what such a life and character would look like has already been done. All we need to do is to look at what Scripture tells us Jesus Christ was like. The goal is to become like Christ.

Paul talks about the old sinful self that we need to take off, and the new self that we have to put on. One way to think about the selves we put off and put on is in terms of character traits—virtues and vices. Vices are the bad habits and practices we are taking off; virtues are the good habits and practices we are putting on. The shift from a vice to a virtue is one part of the rhythm of dying to the old self and rising to the new.

We have been equipped by the Holy Spirit with the power to do this. But participating in the work of Christian formation—being re-formed into the likeness of Christ—over a lifetime is something *we* have to do, and do intentionally. The Holy Spirit is not our fairy godmother, waving her magic wand while we rest on the couch watching TV. Just as we have to take time to pray and read the Bible, we also have to take time to check and double-check our patterns of thought, and desire, and behavior. We have to practice new ways of embodying a more Christlike way of life. Our re-formation will affect the language we use, when and how we eat, what we watch on TV, where and when we shop, our work and our sleep—in short, every area of our lives.

When I was in graduate school, I struggled with what a colleague later dubbed "Imposter Syndrome." I felt inadequate, unprepared, unqualified. Even though I appeared to be doing well, I felt like it was just a matter of time until I was exposed in disgrace as a hopeless case. Years later, I read the medieval theologian Thomas Aquinas on the vice of *pusillanimity*. I discovered that those afflicted with this problem shrink back from all God wants them to be. Like Moses when faced with God's call, they are convinced of their ineptitude and stutter their excuses, instead of trusting God to see them through the work to which they are called.

Learning about this vice was like looking at myself in the mirror for the first time. I stepped back and saw myself through new eyes; I had a name for my weakness. Ironically, knowing my vices became the key to my liberation from them.

> **(Word Alert)**
>
> *Pusillanimity* is an old and seldom-used word that's hard to spell and even harder to pronounce. It means, literally, small-souled. A pusillanimous person cowardly shrinks back from the high calling of God and is content with mediocrity. The opposite is to be magnanimous, or large-souled.

Naming and understanding our vices first helps us know ourselves—this is the "diagnostic" stage. It also helps us better equip ourselves to work against the grain of our sinful nature and to build better character in its place—that is the "treatment" stage. "To flee vice is the beginning of virtue," as one author put it.

The goal, says Paul, is not to beat ourselves up for being bad, but rather to be intentional about building Christlike character. Jesus, our brother, exemplifies the good qualities with which we are trying to clothe ourselves. To become a disciple is to discipline ourselves to be like him.

Now we stand in the gap between who we are and who God calls us to become. Knowing better what holds us back may help us break free. The tradition of self-examination and confession built around the seven deadly sins was designed for just this purpose.

Think It Over

Think of three good qualities of character you see in yourself (virtues or positive traits). Then think of three bad qualities of character (vices or bad habits). Think about ways to break down your bad habits and build up your good ones. How might you intentionally try to re-form your character?

In Other Words

"Pusillanimity is a dangerous habit to acquire because through it we not only lose our taste for what is truly good, but also grow comfortable with mediocrity. [Such a person] never has to grow, never has to change or be challenged because he avoids any goals or commitments that would call him beyond himself in sacrifice, goodness, or love."

—Paul Wadell, *Happiness and the Christian Moral Life*

Live It Out

Write the speech that would be given at your funeral if you were to die right now. Then turn the paper over and write what you wish that speech would have said. In light of what you wrote, how should your goals and priorities change? What should you keep on practicing that is already working well?

A Substitute for Happiness 2

"I am the vine; you are the branches. If you remain in me and I in you, you will bear much fruit; apart from me you can do nothing. If you do not remain in me, you are like a branch that is thrown away and withers; such branches are picked up, thrown into the fire and burned. If you remain in me and my words remain in you, ask whatever you wish, and it will be done for you. This is to my Father's glory, that you bear much fruit, showing yourselves to be my disciples."

—John 15:5-8

This book will focus on the "seven deadly sins" and the virtues opposed to them. The first question people usually ask about the seven deadly sins is, "Why these seven?"

In his book *Wicked Pleasures* Robert Solomon comments, "Real human viciousness and brutality—cruelty, savagery, indifference to human suffering, tyranny, ethnic hatred, religious persecution, and racial bigotry—don't even make the list. . . . Among the man-made evils in the world, the 'deadly' sins barely jiggle the scales of justice, and it hard to imagine why God would bother to raise a celestial eyebrow about them; in other words, why they would rate as sins at all. . . . We are still left with the odd portrait of a God of infinite concerns and capacities being bothered by a bloke who

can't get out of bed [sloth], or takes one too many peeks at a naughty Playboy pictorial [lust], or scarfs down three extra jelly doughnuts [gluttony], or has a nasty thought about his neighbor [envy]" (*Wicked Pleasures: Meditations on the Seven Deadly Sins*, Rowman & Littlefield Pub., Inc. 2006).

Word Alert

The *seven deadly sins*—vainglory, lust, envy, greed, sloth, anger, and gluttony—is a list that goes way back in church history. It's an attempt to identify the fundamental sins from which so much of the wreckage of evil comes.

Why single out these seven, then? The first thing to note is that they are *not* meant to single out the worst of all sins. The original label for the list was the "principle vices" or "the capital vices" because they picked out the sinful habits that were the *sources* of other sins. The idea was to discern deep patterns of thought, feeling, and behavior rather than to pick out an individual action or discrete moment of "sin," in other words, to get to the ultimate psychological roots of sin.

What fears and desires dominate large swaths of our behavior and motivate habitual temptations and failings? Members of the early church practiced self-examination based on the seven vices in an attempt to get to the root of sinful motivation their lives.

Early Christian thinkers pictured the vices as a tree or a spring. The root and trunk of the tree, which grows and nourishes the branches, is pride. The main branches are the seven vices, and each branch vice bears its own poison fruit. Or the wellspring of all sin is pride, and the seven are the main rivers fed by it, and they spread sin's pollution to their respective tributaries and all that relies on that water for life. The idea is that you can pick fruit or dam up tributaries forever, but if you don't get to their source or root, you are fighting a losing battle. The seven vices are an attempt to identify the interior sources of sin, not to put Band-Aids on surface wounds.

Looked at this way, sins are not isolated moments, but parts of a network—a tangle of motivations and actions that have a common source or root. So for example, my temptation to cheat on my taxes (fraud) is the fruit of my excessive desire to secure my own material well-being for myself (avarice), which is in turn a symptom of my desire to make myself happy without relying on or trusting God (pride).

Thomas Aquinas explains that these seven vices are singled out because they concern areas of life we think will give us happiness. Since everyone wants to be happy, and pride motivates us to provide happiness for ourselves on our own terms, these areas are the places sin is easily nourished and fostered. *Greed* concerns money; *lust* concerns pleasure and human sexual relationships; *envy* concerns self-worth and esteem from others; *gluttony* concerns pleasure and bodily preservation; *anger* concerns honor and getting what we deserve; *vainglory* concerns being known and loved by others; and *sloth* concerns commitment and the work we need to sustain it.

Why are we drawn to gluttony or to greed, or to any of the other vices? Because they promise us pleasure and secure provision, and a life of pleasure and secure provision looks like the good life, the life that will make us happy.

Think It Over

1. If you had to pick one of the seven vices to describe your own habitual areas of weakness, which one would it be? How does it function as a substitute for happiness for you?

2. Which vice or vices do you think our culture fosters most? How has the church or Scripture helped you resist it?

In Other Words

"Greed, gluttony, lust, envy, [and] pride are no more than sad efforts to fill the empty place where love belongs, and anger and sloth [are] just two things that may happen when you find that not even all seven of them at their deadliest ever can."

—Frederick Buechner, *Whistling in the Dark*

Live It Out

As you go through the week, try to match an example from popular culture—a film, a novel, a TV show, or a song—with each sin.

Pride: The Queen of the Vices 3

*"Trust in the L*ORD *with all your heart and lean not on your own understanding; in all your ways submit to him, and he will make your paths straight."*

—Proverbs 3:5-6

"We do not dare to classify or compare ourselves with some who commend themselves. When they measure themselves by themselves and compare themselves with themselves, they are not wise. We, however, will not boast beyond proper limits, but will confine our boasting to the sphere of service God himself has assigned to us, a sphere that also includes you."

—2 Corinthians 10:12-13

When I first began to focus on the seven deadly sins, my departmental colleagues teasingly dubbed me the department "Vice Lord." Given that I'm female, however, I told them to call me "Queen of the Vices" instead. Either way, the title is not much of a compliment! Queen of the vices is the traditional name for pride (probably because the Latin name for pride—*superbia*—is a feminine noun). The question is, Why does pride get "pride of place" among the vices?

The basic definition of pride is "having an over-inflated sense of your own worth." Thomas Aquinas calls it "the excessive desire for your own excellence. "To excel," according to the dictionary, means "to be superior to, to surpass in accomplish-

ment or achievement." Being good is not the aim of the prideful person. Nor is being the best you can be. The aim of pride is being *better than everyone else*.

Prideful people crave outranking everyone in goodness, power, and worth. Part of the allure of being number one is that you get to set the standards, you have the power to have things your own way. And we all know how good that feels. It is this aspect of pride—having control to the point of absolute independence—that earns pride its title as queen. For this desire is the ultimate pattern of all sin and vice.

St. Augustine tells a story about his teenage years. He and his friends were bored one night. When one of them suggested stealing pears from the neighbor's pear tree, they snuck onto the neighbor's property, loaded their arms up with as many pears as they could carry, and ran off laughing—only to throw the pears to the pigs. We probably laugh picturing them doing it. A teenage prank, a couple of stolen pears—no real harm done, right?

What was so fun about stealing? Augustine asks himself. Really, he says, what gave him the rush was not getting approval from his friends or the desire for the pears. It was sinning and getting away with it. That made him feel like he was bigger than the law—out of the reach of the police, even out of God's reach. He got to decide what to do without submitting to God's moral order. The fun was in being number one and leaving God out of the picture.

Of course, this is only a sham sort of control. We can't really decide what to do, as if God's laws against stealing don't exist. We can pretend we are powerful enough to make the moral law for ourselves, as Augustine did, but this is just a short-lived fantasy. A life of stealing won't make our life fulfilling and good, even if we want it to. But sometimes the "rush" of pride is enough to convince us to live this fantasy for more than a Friday night with our friends.

All the vices follow the pattern of pride—the pattern of being in control of what is good and what makes us happy. All the vices refuse to submit to what God says is good. When we fall into vice, we are trying to make life good for ourselves on our own.

What is greed but an attempt to provide for ourselves without having to trust or rely on God to give us good things? What is envy but an attempt to rearrange the rankings of worth and goodness so we come out higher than our rival? What is sloth but an attempt to walk away from the disciplined life God calls us to and opt for something we think is easier and more comfortable? What is gluttony but the attempt to cram ourselves full of some fleeting pleasure rather than to wait patiently for real joy that leaves us fulfilled? What is wrath but an attempt to take vengeance for ourselves and set things right on our own terms, rather than to submit to God's plan for justice? What is vainglory but an attempt to pump up our own image rather than letting God's knowledge of and love for us be enough? And what is lust but an attempt to use another person for one's own sexual gratification, rather than as a God-given means to express love and oneness?

Pride is the attempt to create our own happiness. It is not only a sin, but the sin that lies behind all the other vices' attempts to create happiness without God. This queen thinks she has the power to find fulfillment without God. And thus she corrupts all the use of all other good things in service of her twisted end.

Think It Over

Look at the story of David and Bathsheba (2 Sam. 11-12). Discuss how David's lust also fit the pattern of pride.

In Other Words

"Ninety-nine percent of us are addicted to something, whether it is eating, shopping, blaming, or taking care of other people. The simplest definition of an addiction is anything we use to fill the empty place inside of us that belongs to God alone."

—Barbara Brown Taylor, *Home By Another Way*

Live It Out

Write this quote from Mother Teresa on an index card: "In this life we cannot do great things. We can only do small things with great love." Put the card somewhere you will notice it often throughout the day (on the refrigerator door, or posted to your computer screen, or in your pocket) and commit to reading this quote out loud every morning and evening for a week (or at every meal). End each day by thanking the Lord for whatever small things you have done with great love, rather than the "important" things you have accomplished.

Vainglory: Appearance, Attention, Approval 4

"Be careful not to do your 'acts of righteousness' in front of others, to be seen by them. If you do, you will have no reward from your Father in heaven. So when you give to the needy, do not announce it with trumpets, as the hypocrites do in the synagogues and on the streets, to be honored by others. Truly I tell you, they have received their reward in full. But when you give to the needy, do not let your left hand know what your right hand is doing, so that your giving may be in secret. Then your Father, who sees what is done in secret, will reward you.

"And when you pray, do not be like the hypocrites, for they love to pray standing in the synagogues and on the street corners to be seen by others. Truly I tell you, they have received their reward in full. But when you pray, go into your room, close the door, and pray to your Father, who is unseen. Then your Father, who sees what is done in secret, will reward you."

—Matthew 6:1-6

The usual list of seven deadly sins includes pride, envy, sloth, avarice (or greed), anger, lust, and gluttony. Originally, however, the list had eight items—it also included "vainglory." We now tend to identify vainglory with pride. How are they different? And why did the earliest Desert Fathers in the fourth century—the ones who *invented* the list—think it was important to distinguish the two?

> ## Word Alert
> During the fourth century, the desert areas around Egyptian cities attracted people who believed they could better obey their calling to follow Christ by living in solitude. Eventually they introduced some aspects of community living (such as common prayer and meals) that evolved into Christian monasticism. These *Desert Fathers* developed a reputation for holiness and wisdom; their spirituality continues to influence the western church.

In the earliest lists, the sins were listed in order from those most centered around physical desires (lust and gluttony) to those most centered around spiritual desires. Vainglory and pride fell into this latter category. They were considered more dangerous than all the others combined.

Pride, as we have seen, is the excessive desire for preeminence and the power to play God. Like pride, vainglory also concerns excellence, but indirectly. What vainglory wants is not excellence itself, but the *appearance* of excellence and all the social approval that comes with it. Vainglory wants the *image* of beauty. It wants the right people to notice. This beauty may be only skin-deep, but the vainglorious person is determined to manufacture it for herself. Vainglory is the "AAA" vice: Appearance for Attention and Approval. Image is everything.

Vainglory literally means "empty of glory." When we have the vice of vainglory, we are glorying in what is vain or unworthy of glory.

The four main forms of vainglory, identified as far back as the sixth century, sound eerily familiar today:

- Seeking glory for qualities we only pretend to have: pseudo-accomplishments on embellished resumes, exaggerated stories of our past athletic feats, our perfect tan or hair color or complexion (qualities we assume only after the right cosmetics are applied!).

- Seeking glory for things that have no real or lasting worth: our carefully cultivated lawn, our youthful appearance, our snazzy car. These things may mean a lot to us now, but from an eternal perspective they have very little worth.

- Seeking glory by doing things that are wrong: winning laughs by ridiculing others, treating women in ways that get locker-room credit, or even committing crimes—as Augustine did—by stealing or vandalizing.

- Seeking glory by putting on a good Christian "show": through our tireless volunteerism at church, our model children, our moving words in public prayer.

As Jesus notes in the passage above, the worst form of vainglory is reserved for Christians who are trying to do good in order to keep all the glory for themselves. This form of vainglory can spoil every other virtuous thing we do and make us hypocrites. "Every good and perfect gift is from above, coming down from the Father," writes the apostle James (1:17). Any good we do is ultimately a gift from God. Johann Sebastian Bach is remembered for writing *Soli Deo Gloria*—to God be the glory—on each musical score he composed. What does the "score" of *our* lives say?

When we win the approval and applause of others through vainglory, we do not find what we really seek. The sad truth is that our creative ploys to get attention and approval from others can't give us the peace we need. Only God knows us and loves as we are—from the inside out.

Think It Over

Try to think of one vainglorious pursuit that fits each of the four categories discussed above in your own life. How much of what you do throughout the day is driven by the need for attention and approval for others? What did you do today for which God would say, "Well done, good and faithful servant"?

In Other Words

"I lust after recognition, I am desperate to win all the little merit badges and trinkets of my profession, and I am of less real use in this world than any good cleaning lady."

—Garrison Keillor, *Good Poems*

Live It Out

Vainglory, as we've learned, is our attempt to seek approval from others for the things we do. Overcome that tendency by giving God the glory for the good things in your life—pray through a psalm or hymn of praise, or, if you're artistically inclined, create a work of art that depicts God's glory in some way!

Relying on God's Power 5

*"His divine power has given us everything we
need for a godly life through our knowledge of
him who called us by his own glory and goodness.
Through these he has given us his very great and
precious promises, so that through them you may
participate in the divine nature, having escaped the
corruption in the world caused by evil desires.*

*For this very reason, make every effort to add to your
faith goodness; and to goodness, knowledge; and to
knowledge, self-control; and to self-control, perseverance; and to perseverance, godliness; and to godliness, mutual affection; and to mutual affection, love.
For if you possess these qualities in increasing measure, they will keep you from being ineffective and
unproductive in your knowledge of our Lord Jesus
Christ. But if any of you do not have them, you are
nearsighted and blind, and you have forgotten that
you have been cleansed from your past sins.*

*Therefore, my brothers and sisters, make every effort
to confirm your calling and election. For if you do*

these things, you will never stumble, and you will
receive a rich welcome into the eternal kingdom
of our Lord and Savior Jesus Christ."

—2 Peter 1:3-11

From the beginning, the tradition of the seven deadly sins was embedded in a life of spiritual discipline, a life dedicated to becoming more faithful disciples of Jesus Christ. To join this tradition is to benefit from a time-tested way of participating in regular self-examination and confession

> **Word Alert**
>
> In biology, *regeneration* refers to the ability of an organism to grow a new part if the original is lost or broken, as in the ability of a starfish to regenerate a missing leg. Spiritually, regeneration refers to the process by which the Holy Spirit makes us into new persons after the pattern of Jesus Christ.

that leads to regeneration and renewal. But we should recognize that there are dangers along this path too.

The first danger is to lapse into a "works righteousness" mindset: "The harder I work at the spiritual disciplines, the better Christian I will become." Or, "Reflecting constantly on these areas of weakness will make me feel guiltier and guiltier, and that will be a good motivator for all these daily practices."

One pastor I know said that her early sermons ended with too much practical application and not enough grace. Rereading them later, she says, her parting words to the congregation were like a coach before the big game, "OK, everyone, you know what you have to do—GO TEAM!"

Especially when we are struggling with sin and find our own efforts failing time and time again, this sort of call to spiritual discipline can be discouraging and lead us to give up. Not to mention that it promotes the false idea that our efforts can make us somehow more worthy to be saved.

The other danger is to lapse into a "cheap grace" mentality. "I'm justified. Christ covered all my sin with his blood, so I'm OK with God and don't need to be more holy." Or, "No matter what I do, God will forgive me, so it doesn't really matter if I keep on sinning." If we feel that being made right with God is a done deal, we're likely to neglect our focus on discipleship as a lifelong task of growing in the relationship with God that Christ's salvation makes possible.

In the passage above, Peter reminds us that God gives us his Spirit so we can increase in godliness. But we can only do so because "his divine power has given us everything we need" to take on this task. The Spirit is the great enabler; but that means there is something the Spirit empowers us *for*. Peter adds, "Therefore, *brothers and sisters*," making it clear that this is a project we engage in together as a *community* of disciples, as the whole body of Christ together. We are transformed as a body, not just as individual believers.

The key to a life of spiritual discipline is to recognize that God has already equipped us for this great work of transformation. God never asks anything of us that he does not already supply. The difference between a life dedicated to godliness and a life that meanders in spiritual mediocrity is constant dependence on God's Spirit.

Before we examine ourselves, we need to acknowledge that the wisdom to do so comes from God. Before we confess, we need to acknowledge that God delights in our coming to receive healing. And before we engage in these disciplines to root out our deepest sins, we need to rely fully on God's power to combat sin. As surely as sin is entrenched in our lives, God's divine power "has given us everything needed for life and godliness." We dare to confess our sin and seek to root it out step by step, secure in that promise.

Think It Over

1. How has your attitude toward Christian discipleship formed you?

2. What sorts of attitudes and practices does your church community currently foster? Too much complacency, too much effort, or something in between?

In Other Words

"Direct us, O Lord, in all our doings with your most gracious favor, and further us with your continual help; that in all our works begun, continued, and ended in you, we may glorify your holy Name, and finally, by your mercy, obtain everlasting life; through Jesus Christ our Lord. Amen."

—*The Book of Common Prayer*

Live It Out

Take some time today to note your own approach to discipleship. Does it tend toward a sort of "works righteousness" and merit system, or toward an easygoing "God will forgive and accept me anyway" approach? Pray for the Spirit's power to help you rely on God's power to overcome sin in your life.

The Roots and Branches of Sin
Discussion Guide

You've probably heard of the seven deadly sins—maybe you can even name a couple of them. If you're like most people, the term sounds old-fashioned, and, well, depressing. Let's face it, meditating on our sins doesn't sound very inviting. But this list of sins has a long and useful history in the Christian church. It's meant to help us understand how sin operates in our lives so that we can overcome it.

If you bring your car to a garage, the mechanic isn't going to ask you how great it's performing. The question is, What's wrong? You're going to describe how it loses power on hills or the strange vibration coming from the front end. The mechanic will ask more questions about when that happens and what it sounds like. Somewhere there's a root cause, and in a car, it's typically either the electrical system or the fuel system.

Thinking about the seven deadly sins is like bringing your car to a mechanic. These sins are used as an aid in self-examination and confession—practices essential to becoming more faithful followers of Christ. The sins—or, as they're sometimes called, the capital vices—are a way of describing the "old selves" that have to die in order for our new, Christ-like selves to born. This rhythm of confession and regeneration, dying and rising, is the work of the Holy Spirit in us, and it is our work too.

The seven deadly sins are called "capital vices" because you can trace them to their source. They're rooted in pride, the ultimate source of sin. And because they channel pride's desire for control into all areas of our lives, they incite us to many other sins in the process. The seven—vainglory, envy, anger, gluttony, sloth, greed (avarice), and lust (with pride as their root)—aren't meant to pick out the worst or even the most common sins. Rather, they point to areas of our lives in which our desires tend to resist God, in which we try to make ourselves happy all on our own.

> **Word Alert**
>
> In ancient times the *vices* were pictured as a tree whose root was pride, whose branches were the seven capital vices, and whose poison fruit were the sins that grew from these branches. It was a picture of a network of related sins that gave people insight into the deepest roots of sin in their lives.

Pride and vainglory are both sins concerned with the sort of excellence, or stand-out status, that gains us power and recognition. It is worth asking why we so often try to acquire power and recognition for ourselves. Do our habits and patterns of thought show how much we trust God, or how much we are still trying to keep things under our own control?

Ice Breakers

(15 minutes—give or take)

If this is a new group meeting for the first time, **take some time to get acquainted.** Invite group members to give their name and then mention something that they are really proud of—in a good way!

Option

If that seems too gimmicky, just go around the circle and introduce yourselves. Invite everyone to complete the statement "Happiness is. . . ."

If this is a continuing group, take a few minutes to regroup. **If there are any new members, everyone should briefly introduce themselves** as in the option above.

For Starters

(5 minutes)

Invite group members to briefly share one insight they gained from the devotional readings. Don't discuss it now, just mention it.

Let's Focus

(5 minutes)

Review the introduction to this session, and then have someone read this focus statement aloud:

Looking at the seven deadly sins (or capital vices) is a foundation to exploring the spiritual disciplines we need to die to our "old selves" and grow a more Christlike character. All seven share a common root in pride, our constant impulse to be independent from God. We can use them for self-examination and confession, discovering the ways our deepest desires are still formed by sinful habits. Empowered by the Holy Spirit, we can then move toward re-forming our character in ways that are more like Christ.

Word Search

(20 minutes)

Discuss the following Scripture passages (or, if you're running short on time, choose the ones the group wants to discuss):

- Colossians 3:1-14
  What does it mean to "set our minds" on things above?

  What does it mean to "set our hearts" on things above?

  Why do you think Paul says both?

  What parts of our lives are emphasized in Paul's description of the ways of the "old self" and the "new self"? Why?

- Genesis 3:1-7
  How does this story of "original sin" depict pride?

What do you think it means that Adam and Eve wanted to be "like God?"

In what ways is that same desire expressed in your own life?

- Romans 12:1-2
  What is the motive for what Paul calls our "living sacrifice?"

  How does offering this "living sacrifice" move us toward reversing the desire to be like God?

Bring It Home
(20 minutes, or as time allows)

Choose *one* of the following options.

Option 1
Using newsprint or a board, ask a volunteer to **draw the "tree of vices" (see Word Alert in the Introduction to this session) with its root of pride and the poisonous fruits of sin they produce.** Discuss together how pride is the source of each of the seven deadly sins as you understand them.

Option 2
As time permits, choose from among the following questions and discuss them:

- We sometimes say to children or friends, "I'm so proud of you," or we "take pride in" some part of our heritage. What is this "good" kind of pride, and why is it good? (See Gal. 6:4.) How is it different from sinful pride?

- Most of us can identify proud people who strut about and call attention to themselves. What are some of the more subtle forms of pride that operate in your life?

- Jesus said about our giving (or any virtuous act), "Do not let your left hand know what your right hand is doing" (Matt. 6:3). What are some of the ways you can fight against the "vainglory" of even good acts?

Option 3
Listen to Tobymac's "All In" (from the CD *Portable Sounds*) together. What do you think is one thing that you need to "let go of" in order to be "all in" as a disciple of Christ?

Pray It Through
(10 minutes)

Take time to suggest items to pray about together.

Hopefully you will see yourselves more clearly, with the Spirit's guidance, and can encourage each other in the daily disciplines that enable us to be more Christlike. Share one thing you've learned in this session that you'd like the others to pray for. Then pray for the person next to you (left or right). End with this prayer (from *The Book of Common Prayer*) in unison:

"Direct us, O Lord, in all our doings, with your most gracious favor, and further us with your continual help; that in all our works begun, continued, and ended in you, we may glorify your holy name, and finally, by your mercy, obtain everlasting life, through Jesus Christ our Lord, Amen."

Option
Or invite group members to share prayer requests or thanksgivings. Then pray for each other in any way that feels comfortable for the group.

Live It Out
(all week)

To help uproot vainglory, try practicing the special discipline of silence for a day or for the entire week. Try to avoid talking about yourself at all. When others criticize you or you feel the need to say something to bolster your image or defend yourself, make the choice to refrain from intervening. Instead, try to be a good and accepting listener to others. As you practice this discipline, notice any changes in your attitudes or relationships that happen as a result.

> ### Web Alert
>
> **Be sure to check out the participants' section for this session on www.GrowDisciples.org for interesting links and suggestions for readings and activities that will deepen your understanding of the sin of vainglory.**

Session 2
Envy

Winners and Losers 1

"Now Israel loved Joseph more than any of his other sons, because he had been born to him in his old age; and he made a richly ornamented robe for him. When his brothers saw that their father loved him more than any of them, they hated him and could not speak a kind word to him."

—Genesis 37:3-4

The film *Amadeus* is the story of Antonio Salieri, a composer in eighteenth-century Vienna. It is also a story of envy and the way it consumes us.

As a young boy, Salieri had prayed for God to give him the gift of music and an audience who would appreciate that gift. Instead, Mozart arrives on the scene and steals everyone's attention with his huge talent. Even Mozart's name galls Salieri: Wolfgang *Amadeus* Mozart, meaning "loved by God." Salieri blames God for lavishing musical gifts on the ungrateful Mozart instead of answering Salieri's own prayers. Unable to stand the humiliation of being constantly outshone by Mozart, Salieri arranges circumstances that bring about his rival's death at an early age.

Years later Salieri, who has become a bitter old man stricken with guilt and self-hatred over his part in Mozart's death, attempts suicide. When a priest arrives to hear his confession, Salieri plays tune after tune he has written, expecting that one of them will be familiar to his listener. But the priest shakes his head again and again, embarrassed that he does not recognize a single one. Only when Salieri plays a sparkling little tune by his rival Mozart does the priest light up in recognition.

Compared to Mozart's musical genius, Salieri knows, he will always be second-best—and second-rate.

Like Salieri and like Joseph's brothers, we desperately want to be loved and affirmed. A rival who steals that love and affirmation robs us of something we deeply *need*. And so Salieri's jealousy of Mozart is not as much about musical talent as it is about being recognized and affirmed by God as worthy of love. Joseph's brothers don't really want nicer coats—instead they crave their father's love.

Don't we all?

That's why envy makes perfect sense to us. And yet it is also irrational. For those who are envious see the love and worth they need as something for which they have to compete with others. Only if we outrank another can we earn it. We seem to think that our rival's superior skill or position or talent automatically disqualifies us from attaining that love and sense of worth.

Like Joseph's brothers, not all of us are loved fully and loved equally. In our world there are winners and losers: those who are more worthy and those who are less worthy, those who are superior and those who are inferior. We define ourselves by being "better than . . ."

Thomas Aquinas defines envy as "being unhappy about another's good because it exceeds your own." Depending on what we value in ourselves and want to be loved for, we may compete in different arenas than others, and envy different rivals. But wherever we stand, it's easy to feel as if we're living in a competition where the stakes are high.

We envy others who threaten our worth because we mistakenly believe our worthiness is conditional on how we measure up against others. These comparisons reveal our inferiority; they show what we lack. And sadly, when we envy another, we despise ourselves as well as our rival.

Think It Over

Think of a time when you were envious of someone? Why did you envy him or her, and what impact did the envy have on you?

In Other Words

"Envy . . . moves from dejection to disparagement to destruction. It is not so much the looking up as the bringing down."

—Os Guiness, *Steering Through Chaos*

Live It Out

Envy causes us to despise ourselves as well as our rivals. Try this: next time you feel envious of another person, perhaps at work, think about how you will respond. For example, instead of griping about this person's success to a friend, try congratulating her or writing her a note. Notice how this action makes you feel about yourself.

Poison Fruit 2

"Surely God is good to Israel, to those who are pure in heart. But as for me, my feet had almost slipped; I had nearly lost my foothold. For I envied the arrogant when I saw the prosperity of the wicked. They have no struggles; their bodies are healthy and strong. They are free from common human burdens; they are not plagued by human ills. Therefore pride is their necklace; they clothe themselves with violence. From their callous hearts comes iniquity; the evil conceits of their minds know no limits. They scoff, and speak with malice; with arrogance they threaten oppression. Their mouths lay claim to heaven, and their tongues take possession of the earth. Therefore their people turn to them and drink up waters in abundance. They say, 'How would God know? Does the Most High know anything?' This is what the wicked are like—always free of care, they go on amassing wealth."

—Psalm 73:1-12

What does envy look like? Obviously envy begins to fester in the heart and then shows itself outwardly. But what are its usual symptoms?

St. Augustine's Prayer Book, a twentieth-century manual for confession, includes this list of envious behaviors:

- Offense at the talents, success, or good fortune of others
- Selfish or unnecessary rivalry or competition
- Pleasure at others' difficulties or distress
- Belittling others
- Ill-will
- False accusations
- Slander (publicly saying something bad, even if true, about someone)
- Backbiting (doing the same, but behind his or her back)
- Reading false motives into others' behavior
- Initiation, collection, or retelling of gossip
- Arousing, fostering, or organizing antagonism against others
- Unnecessary criticism, even when true
- Teasing or bullying
- Scorn of another's virtue, ability, shortcomings, or failings
- Prejudice against those we consider inferior, or who consider us inferior or who seem to threaten our security or position
- Ridicule of persons, institutions, or ideals

Although perhaps there are others, these are classic symptoms of an envious heart. They describe the way we act when envy dominates our lives. It is a little disconcerting to discover how many of them are a frequent part of our daily behavior.

In the Christian tradition, the "poison fruit" of envy includes unhappiness when another does well, and, ultimately, hatred of others and God. Perhaps you think "hatred of God" sounds a little extreme. But scorning and despising the people God has made and the gifts God has given is a shorter step than you might realize to scorning and despising the Creator.

Envy, in short, leads us to belittle others, to seek evil for them, and even to try to take them down ourselves. Notice from the items on the list above that envy is often expressed verbally: gossip and backbiting fall into this category. Put-downs are the bread and butter of TV sitcoms, and many of us have perfected the art of putting others down in our own lives as well. Is it just for laughs, or do we actually take pleasure in this behavior? When children tease or bully each other, it's usually obvious that they do so out of a lack of self-esteem or self-respect. When adults do this, their lack of self-love may be less obvious but is no less real.

Thomas Aquinas teaches that envy is the opposite of the virtue of Christian love. Love for God includes love for our neighbor (as we love ourselves). Just as these three loves go naturally together, so do the opposite three hatreds. As the story of Salieri so clearly demonstrates, the person who envies does not love himself, and this self-loathing quickly turns outward, making the person unable to love his or her neighbor. This inability to love our neighbor always affects our ability to love God. So envy leads to a vicious spiral of hating—in which everyone, perhaps most of all the person who envies, gets hurt.

Think It Over

Think of a rivalry—either from your own experience or from a novel or movie—that destroyed the people in it. Then try to think of a rivalry that raised the competitors to a new level of excellence. What made the difference?

In Other Words

"As a moth gnaws a garment, so doth envy consume a man."

—Saint John Chrysostom, fourth century

Live It Out

Go through the checklist on page 45 and identify the symptoms of envy that are most characteristic in your life. Which ones were your top three? Why? This week, try to avoid your top-ranked symptom. Concentrate instead on increasing your appreciation of God's gifts and love—to yourself and others.

The Enemy of Love 3

> *"But now, this is what the LORD says—he who created you, Jacob, he who formed you, Israel: 'Do not fear, for I have redeemed you; I have summoned you by name; you are mine. When you pass through the waters, I will be with you; and when you pass through the rivers, they will not sweep over you. When you walk through the fire, you will not be burned; the flames will not set you ablaze. For I am the LORD your God, the Holy One of Israel, your Savior; I give Egypt for your ransom, Cush and Seba in your stead. Since you are precious and honored in my sight, and because I love you, I will give nations in exchange for you, and peoples in exchange for your life.'"*
>
> —Isaiah 43:1-4

"Of all the seven deadly sins," writes Joseph Epstein, "only envy is no fun at all." Envy creates malice between us and others; it causes us to resent God; and it causes our own sense of inferiority and inadequacy to fester.

In his book *Envy: The Seven Deadly Sins*, Epstein tells the following story:

[A]n Englishwoman, a Frenchman, and a Russian . . . are each given a wish by one of those genies whose . . . habit it is to pop out of bottles. The Englishwoman says that a friend of hers had a charming cottage in the Cotswolds, and that she would like a similar cottage, with the addition of two extra bedrooms and a second bath and a brook running in front of it. The Frenchman says that his best friend has a beautiful blonde mistress, and he would like such a mistress himself, but a redhead instead of a blonde and with longer legs and bit more in the way of culture and chic. The Russian, when asked what he would like, tells of a neighbor who has a cow that gives a vast quantity of the richest milk, which yields the heaviest cream and the purest butter. "I vant dat cow," the Russian tells the genie, "dead."

Getting ahead of the rivals we envy is a temporary and a fragile foundation for our self-worth. More often than not, our state of inferiority feels impossible to get rid of, which is why the envious tend to smolder in their resentments and stew in their own spiteful soup.

So how can we escape envy's destructive and joyless hold? What we really need to escape envy is a sense of self-worth, a sense of our goodness and gifts that is not based on conditional comparisons.

We need a new vision of ourselves—one that makes us secure and gives us the freedom to love again. Various secular writers proclaim it to be incurable. They try to spin envy's competitive habits toward more constructive ends like self-improvement. If, on the other hand, envy *is* curable, we will need to look at ourselves through the eyes of God's love for us to find a way out.

Isaiah 43 tells us that God knows us by name. God honors us and loves us. Why? Because we are God's own children. We belong to him. No other reason. No comparative measure. This is unconditional acceptance. Isn't that how we all want to be loved?

"The Christian's self-understanding," explains Robert C. Roberts in his book *Spiritual Emotions*, "is that she is precious before God—however much a sinner, however much a failure (or success) she may be by the standards of worldly comparisons. . . . The message is that God loves me for myself—not for anything I have achieved, not for my beauty or intelligence or righteousness or for any other 'qualification,' but simply in the way that a good mother loves the fruit of her womb. If I can get that into my head—or better, into my heart—then I won't be grasping desperately for self-esteem at the expense of others."

Envy is the enemy of love, and love is the only thing that can save us from it.

Think It Over

Read Psalm 139 and meditate on God's love for you—before you were born, before anyone knew you or judged you, before you did or accomplished anything. Spend five minutes thinking about how it feels to be loved like that, and live the rest of your day out of that confidence.

In Other Words

"Love is patient, love is kind. It does not envy, it does not boast, it is not proud. It does not dishonor others, it is not self-seeking, it is not easily angered, it keeps no record of wrongs. Love does not delight in evil but rejoices with the truth. It always protects, always trusts, always hopes, always perseveres."

—1 Corinthians 13:4-7

Live It Out

Choose a person you work with or regularly associate with in some way. Write down three positive traits or spiritual strengths of this person. Thank God for the blessing of these gifts. Then try to find a way of letting this person know you recognize these qualities in him or her.

Haves and Have-Nots 4

> *"You shall not make for yourself an image in the form of anything in heaven above or on the earth beneath or in the waters below. You shall not bow down to them or worship them; for I, the LORD your God, am a jealous God. . . . You shall not covet your neighbor's wife. You shall not set your desire on your neighbor's house or land, his male or female servant, his ox or donkey, or anything that belongs to your neighbor."*
>
> —Deuteronomy 5:8-9a, 21

Envy is easily confused with other sins like jealousy. In everyday conversation we often use these terms interchangeably: "You're going to Hawaii for a three-week vacation? I'm so jealous!"

The jealous person is distinguished from the envious person by whether she is a *have*, rather than a *have-not*. Jealousy flares when someone threatens to take something good away from us. In its righteous form, as in the passage above describing God's desire for fidelity and exclusive worship from his people, jealousy is rooted in justice—in what is rightfully ours.

Jealousy's bad name comes from its selfish, paranoid, and harmful forms: as when a jealous man keeps the woman he "loves" under his control, treats her like his property, or harms another person to get her back. Notice that God's possessive claim on us—"You are mine!"—is not appropriate for human beings to have toward another.

Unlike those who are jealous, covetous people are in the position of *have-nots*. To covet our neighbor's house requires that we do not have the beautiful house they *do* have. Covetousness is primarily about possessions. The covetous person wants something she does not have, and is most concerned with getting it for herself. If that means taking it away from another person, so be it. Her main intent, however, is not to harm another but to acquire something for herself.

Greedy people may want possessions too, but they want more, or enough to feel secure, or to have one just like their neighbor. The premise of covetousness—*like* envy and *unlike* greed—is wanting *the very one* you have, not merely one just like yours. Think, for example of Ahab's desire for Naboth's vineyard (1 Kings 20).

As with covetousness, the person who envies also starts from a position of *not-having.* But in this case, the lack is linked to self-esteem—the ability to love and value ourselves and to recognize and accept unconditional love from others. Not having something does not just leave the envious person wanting that thing. Instead it leaves him feeling inferior, as if he is personally deficient or defective for not having, or for having less.

This lack makes the envious person feel less lovable, less admirable, less of a person. For that reason envy is usually personal. It's about love and identity, unlike the possession-oriented vices of greed and covetousness. So greed and covetousness can lead to stealing; envy and jealousy to personal harm. Joseph's brothers didn't just tear off his coat—they sold him into slavery to get rid of him forever (Gen. 37 ff.).

It is important to recognize that envy is really about our need for love and our understanding that love has an unconditional form. Its connection to love makes envy a serious sin, one that both reflects and inflicts serious damage on the

human heart. In Aquinas's treatment of the vices, envy and sloth are the only two opposed to the theological virtue of *agape* love. Envy isn't just a twisted or perverted love of something less than God, but the inability to love and accept love at all.

Think It Over

Look at Hosea 3 for a picture of God's relationship to Israel and his demands for fidelity. Does God's jealousy look different when we see that he is willing to lay down his life for her, and that he wins her back so that she can freely return his love? How is this different than the human jealousy we are more familiar with?

In Other Words

"I laugh at men's losses, they lick about my heart,
And I weep at their winnings, and bewail hard times.
And thus I live, loveless, like a lying dog,
And all my body boils, for bitterness of fall."

—Envy, in William Langland's *Visions from Piers Plowman*

Live It Out

Reflect on the times you feel envious and see if it connects with the ability to love and be loved in your own life.

Apprentices 5

> *"For the grace of God has appeared that offers salvation to all people. It teaches us to say 'No' to ungodliness and worldly passions, and to live self-controlled, upright and godly lives in this present age, while we wait for the blessed hope—the appearing of the glory of our great God and Savior, Jesus Christ, who gave himself for us to redeem us from all wickedness and to purify for himself a people that are his very own, eager to do what is good."*
>
> —Titus 2:11-14

Every week as I stand in the check-out lane, not so patiently waiting with my not-so-patient little boys to pay for groceries, I cannot help but examine the long line of tabloid magazines on the rack before us. These publications feed on celebrities, politicians, and notorious criminals. Need a public forum to advertise someone's cellulite, messy divorce, bad hair day, painful lawsuit, or bust for drug abuse? Look no further! Sex sells, but apparently, so does taking delight in others' misfortune. The theme of these magazines, which resonates so well with envious everyday North Americans, is to take people whom we envy—for their fame, their wealth, their beauty, their significant other, or their glamorous lifestyle—and ruin their good name. That is, ruin them.

When I ask my students to name ten celebrities, they have no problem rattling them off—complete with unsolicited derogatory remarks about each. When I ask them to name their heroes, I am usually met first with silence, and then, after some thought, a list of about three. Some of my male high school students cite their grandfather as someone they admire and strive to be like. I hope they told their grandfathers that too! None of their heroes were celebrities; most were family members, coaches, or older members of the church.

Our heroes give us role models to imitate—concrete and earthy pictures of what a Christlike life looks like here and now. They are our local saints, godly figures whose footsteps we can walk in, folks who can show us a hundred different ways to live Jesus' love in all sorts of different circumstances.

> **Word Alert**
>
> *Saints* aren't just the plaster statues that line some churches. Saint simply means "holy person," and Paul uses it to address every person in that rather unruly church at Corinth. Local saints are those people around us who are ahead of us in holiness, and are our examples.

When we envy, we want to tarnish the reputation of those who outshine us. How can we turn envy into genuine admiration? By thinking of ourselves as apprentices rather than detractors or competitors. The saints are not competing with us for acclaim or favor in the eyes of God or of the world. They are there to encourage us and to help us become godlier ourselves (see Heb. 12:1).

To be an apprentice is to admit you have something to learn and plenty of room for improvement. To be envious, on the other hand, is to try to hide your inferiority or spoil your rival's superiority by bringing her down. The other way to level the playing field is to strive to be lifted up yourself. This is the way of grace.

In the end, becoming like Christ is not a competition. If we all become more Christlike, there are no losers—only a group of human beings who experience richer fellowship with God and each other.

Spiritual growth means knowing that we can be better and looking to others who are better than ourselves to imitate. This self-knowledge, unlike envy, is not tainted with self-despising and self-hatred. It is anchored in frank humility.

In humility, we are free to stand firm in God's love and then earnestly desire to be better. Being better isn't a condition of being loved more—by God or by ourselves. And the desire to be better isn't driven by some sense that we need to earn our way in or overcome our inferiority. Instead it is motivated by the kind of love that makes us want to be the best we can be for the One we love, the One who loves us already.

To break out of envy is to found our strivings in the security of love rather than the anxiety that we will never be able to find love. Then we can look toward others as inspiring examples rather than threatening competitors.

What are you zealous for? And who in your life can help show you the way?

Think It Over

Think of a person who has helped you to become a better disciple of Christ. How did this person lead by example, instruction, or encouragement? How did this person make you want to be better?

In Other Words

"The Holy Spirit has been called 'the Lord, the giver of life,' and drawing their power from that source, saints are essentially life-givers. To be with them is to become more alive."

—Frederick Buechner, *Wishful Thinking*

Live It Out

This week, try offering only words of affirmation and encouragement to others. Silence any reputation-ruining talk you might be tempted to speak about them.

Envy
Discussion Guide

The sin of envy centers on our need to be loved. Envy makes us see earning and securing love as a competitive venture. Feeling loved and affirmed as a valuable person depends on how we rank in comparison with others, and there are no prizes for second place. When we're in the grip of envy, we feel inferior. In order to be worth something or to be loved, then, we feel we have to outdo others.

Envy has various strategies, all of which involve belittling others in some way, or "taking them down a peg." We want our rivals to be less than we are, or to have less than we have. In the end, though, these strategies show our lack of love for ourselves, for others, and even for God, whom we blame for unequally doling out the goods that earn us esteem. In the worst cases, envy leads to hatred.

To resist envious patterns and practices in our lives, we need a new vision of ourselves as unconditionally loved by God. Nothing we do or achieve, no qualities that we have or lack, and no comparisons to others can ever change that. If we ground our self-worth on God's love, we can find joy in relationships that genuinely appreciate our own goodness and the goodness of others.

For Starters
(10 minutes)

Warmly welcome anyone who is new to your group. Be sure to "bring them up to speed" by briefly summarizing your last session. The review won't hurt the rest of you either. Allow some time for anyone who wants to report on their experiences this past week with the spiritual discipline of silence (against vainglory). Was this exercise helpful to you? What did you learn about yourself and the pitfalls of your daily life?

Or invite group members to share one insight from the daily devotions that was meaningful for them. Don't discuss it now, just mention it.

Let's Focus
(5 minutes)

Review the introduction to this session, and then have someone read this focus statement aloud:

Envy is about our need to be unconditionally loved. It operates out of a lack—a lack of knowing about that kind of love and a lack of feeling that kind of love from God or accepting it as real and reliable. Envy's connection to love makes it a serious vice, one that both reflects and inflicts serious damage on ourselves, on others, and on our relationship with God. Envy reveals a lack of self-love and self-acceptance. It exhibits itself in us whenever we want to bring others down. Only the unconditional love that God offers can heal an envious heart.

Word Search
(20 minutes)

Discuss the following Scripture passages (or, if you're running short on time, choose the ones the group wants to discuss):

* Genesis 37:1-11
  Robert Roberts defines "spiritual cannibalism" as the quality of relationships in which one person seeks to gain worth at another's expense. Is Joseph's dream-telling an example of this?

* Is the brothers' revenge an example of this?

* Who is playing the comparative game in this family, and why?

What do you think would have helped Joseph's brothers resist their envy?

- Psalm 73
  This Psalm might be titled: "The Anatomy of Envy, and Its Cure." What provokes the psalmist's envy?

  Where does it lead?

  How does he resolve it?

- Luke 1:46-53
  God often reverses the social rankings human beings construct, showing love to those who are inferior and who lack worth or status. What does Mary's song teach us about dealing with envy?

Bring It Home
(20 minutes, or as time allows)

Choose one of the following options.

Option 1
Read James 3:13-18. On a board or a sheet of newsprint make two columns with "Wisdom 1" and "Wisdom 2" at the top. **Make a list of the characteristics of the two kinds of wisdom,** using what James says and adding any you might think of.

Option 2
As time permits, choose from among the following questions and discuss them:

- Share a time in your life when you were envious. What provoked it? How did it affect you? How was it related to your own sense of worth and your trust in God?

- "Keeping up with the Joneses" seems to be a common theme in many people's lives. In your experience, what contributes to this attitude?

- Share a couple of things you've personally found helpful in fighting the sin of envy.

Option 3

Play this guessing game and enjoy the affirmation of love for each person present—a counterpoint to envy! Spend a moment listing three positive qualities of the person sitting next to you on a 3 x 5 card. Write the person's name at the bottom of the card. Then shuffle all the cards and put them in an envelope. Select one card at a time and, without disclosing the name on it, read the traits off one by one. Have the group guess who is the person described.

Pray It Through
(10 minutes)

Take time to suggest items to pray about together.

Remember to also thank God for

- people who have loved you as God loves you—unconditionally—modeling the character of Christ for you and encouraging you in your walk with God.

- God's abundant love for you, rather than a love you are need to earn.

At the end, pray in unison from W. H. Auden's "Many Happy Returns":

"Then, since all self-knowledge tempts us to envy, may we . . . love one another without desiring all that we are not." Amen.

Live It Out
(5-15 minutes each day during the coming week)

At the beginning of each day, read Psalm 73:23-25 aloud. Better yet, write it on an index card (or memorize it) to take with you for the day, and reread it at noon and before bed. The idea is to remind yourself of God's unconditional love for you, and then to live out your day in the comfort of that love. When we feel securely loved for who we are, we are less tempted to indulge in envy.

Web Alert

Be sure to check out the participants' section for this session on www.GrowDisciples.org for interesting links and suggestions for readings and activities that will deepen your understanding of the sin of envy.

Session 3
Wrath

Emotion or Sin?

"You have heard that it was said to the people long ago, 'You shall not murder, and anyone who murders will be subject to judgment.' But I tell you that anyone who is angry with a brother or sister will be subject to judgment. Again, anyone who says to a brother or sister, 'Raca,' is answerable to the Sanhedrin. And anyone who says, 'You fool!' will be in danger of the fire of hell. Therefore, if you are offering your gift at the altar and there remember that your brother or sister has something against you, leave your gift there in front of the altar. First go and be reconciled to that person; then come and offer your gift. Settle matters quickly with your adversary who is taking you to court. Do it while you are still together on the way, or your adversary may hand you over to the judge, and the judge may hand you over to the officer, and you may be thrown into prison. Truly I tell you, you will not get out until you have paid the last penny."

—Matthew 5:21-26

Of the seven deadly sins, the Bible probably has the most to say about greed and wrath. And most of what it says—like Jesus' words above—is negative. But is all anger bad?

From almost the beginning, there has been a dispute in the Christian tradition on just this issue. One side says anger is a natural, healthy, human emotion,

Word Alert

Those who share this view distinguish between *anger* as a psychological feature of human nature and *wrath*, its excessive or misdirected form.

part of the package of emotions that helps us negotiate threats and dangers and preserve ourselves. Anger is not sinful in itself—only when it rages out of control or targets the wrong offenders.

Because anger is the emotional response of those who recognize that they have been wronged, it requires a sense of justice. Anger, at its best, says Aquinas, can energize us to seek justice, as long as we never let anger rage out of control like a wildfire. Furthermore, he says, we are to follow the example of Christ, who experienced a full range of human emotions, from sadness to anger, but who also had the virtue of gentleness.

Other voices in the Christian tradition counsel differently. They say that anger is something we should never feel toward another human being. We can be angry at sin, perhaps, or at evil spirits who tempt us. But anger is so volatile and destructive that it will invariably disturb our prayers and prevent us from properly loving our neighbor.

Proponents of this position say that anger is almost always an irresistible temptation to selfishness. Our anger prompts us to demand something for ourselves that we would never seek for others. It prompts us to protect ourselves and our reputations at the cost of ignoring our own faults, or to exaggerate harm or slights because we think too highly of ourselves. If we were truly selfless, we would not feel the anger we do.

Commenting on Ephesians 4:31: "Get rid of all bitterness, rage and anger, brawling and slander, along with every form of malice," John Cassian, one of the fourth-century Desert Fathers, immediately closes off the obvious loophole: "When [the apostle] says, "All anger should be removed from you," he makes no exception at all for us as to necessity and utility." "All anger" means *all* anger, with the possible exception of anger at our own sin.

There is wisdom in both positions. Although most of us now think of anger as part of a healthy human response to evil in the world, we do well to heed a word about its dangers. Perhaps we will find, after examining the patterns of anger in our own lives, that almost all of it is sinful, selfish anger, and thus laying down almost all anger is a worthwhile discipline for us.

Think It Over

1. Think of the last time you were angry. What situation or who caused your anger? How would you characterize it?

2. Which "side" of the Christian tradition on anger resonates with your own experience? How?

In Other Words

"O God, I am hellishly angry; I think so-and-so is a swine; I am tortured by worry about this or that; I am pretty certain that I have missed my chances in life; this or that has left me feeling terribly depressed. But nonetheless here I am like this, feeling both bloody and bloody-minded, and I am going to stay here for ten minutes.

You are most unlikely to give me anything. I know that. But I am going to stay for the ten minutes nonetheless."

—Harry Williams, from *The HarperCollins Book of Prayers*, compiled by Robert Van de Weyer

Live It Out

Think of an unjust situation that calls for righteous anger: racism, poverty, hunger . . . the list could go on. Then do something constructive about it: write a letter to your local, state, and national representatives, help out at a food bank, participate in local opportunities to fight against the sin of racism.

Holy Anger 2

"Another time Jesus went into the synagogue, and a man with a shriveled hand was there. Some of them were looking for a reason to accuse Jesus, so they watched him closely to see if he would heal him on the Sabbath. Jesus said to the man with the shriveled hand, 'Stand up in front of everyone.' Then Jesus asked them, 'Which is lawful on the Sabbath: to do good or to do evil, to save life or to kill?' But they remained silent. He looked around at them in anger and, deeply distressed at their stubborn hearts, said to the man, 'Stretch out your hand.' He stretched it out, and his hand was completely restored. Then the Pharisees went out and began to plot with the Herodians how they might kill Jesus."

—Mark 3:1-6

This scene in Mark's gospel is a picture of holy anger—Jesus' anger. Jesus sees a human being suffering, and he sees the Pharisees carefully watching his every move. He looks from one to the other, and then he calls the man to come forward. He brings the Pharisees face to face with the man with the withered hand, and he asks them to open their eyes: "You stand up front, clothed in reputations for holiness; this man shrinks in the back pew. But you are both worshiping the same God. You are both God's children. He is suffering." Will the Pharisees let themselves see? Will their eyes

and shoulders drop, along with their religious pretenses? "Where is *love* in this synagogue?" Jesus seems to cry out.

The Pharisees will not answer. They are stubborn, not speechless. Their jaws are set. They look him straight in the eye without blinking, without emotion, without remorse. And Jesus doesn't know whether to rage or to weep at their hardened hearts.

Jesus' anger does not paralyze him or cause him to lash out at them. His course is as firmly set on compassion as their jaws are set in callousness. "Stretch out your hand." Jesus not only heals the man, he heals right under the Pharisees' noses, on their turf, knowing he is breaking their rules. Does he do it in order to thumb his nose at them, to goad them to revenge? No. Rather, he does it to teach them that love does not back down. Love is the fulfillment of the law, not a casualty of the law.

Many people assume that the only record of anger in the gospels is the cleansing of the temple (although John describes Jesus as "zealous"). I'd suggest that this scene from Mark actually teaches us more simply and clearly about holy anger, God's anger. Mark, the most terse gospel writer, spends a full sentence here describing Jesus' emotional reaction in this scene.

Why is Jesus angry? With whom is he angry? How is he angry?

Jesus yearns for the Pharisees to lead by love. He longs for his people to instinctively respond to each other with compassion, without pride or reputation-seeking or legally earned righteousness or any other humanly contrived obstacle. The religious leaders' concern with their own honor has clouded their ability to love those who suffer. Jesus makes them stand face to face with the man with the withered hand. He gives them an opportunity to clear their vision. He invites them to learn to love again. It was one of those moments that could have turned the whole narrative a different direction.

But the Pharisees say no to love and are unrepentant in their refusal. Confronted by their stubbornness, Jesus is angry. He grieves at their hardness of heart like a frustrated parent who catches one of her children hurting another. "Stop! Look at what you are doing—can't you see how you are *hurting* him?" Jesus is angry because he loves the Pharisees and he loves the man with the withered hand, and he knows it doesn't have to be this way. He is angry and grieved all at once because he knows that they are choosing death over life. He longs for them to change their hearts. Jesus' anger expresses his love of others and his love of justice, all wrapped together.

How does he show his anger? He does not retaliate. But neither does he walk away resigned. He stays and heals the man with the withered hand. He looks the religious leaders in the eye and shows them what real love looks like.

Think It Over

Christians are called to imitate Christ—that is, to become like him. How would you describe Jesus' character here in this scene from

Mark? What virtues does he show? What would a Christian life with these virtues look like? Could a Christian ever be a habitually angry person?

In Other Words

"Hate cannot drive out hate: only love can do that."

—Martin Luther King, Jr.

Live It Out

Listen to U2's "Peace on Earth" (on the album *All That You Can't Leave Behind*). Does the frustration with suffering expressed in this song seem like, or unlike, Christ's response? Why?

Out of Control 3

> *"Do not make friends with the hot-tempered, do not associate with those who are easily angered, or you may learn their ways and get yourself ensnared."*
>
> —Proverbs 22:24-25

> *"My dear brothers and sisters, take note of this: Everyone should be quick to listen, slow to speak and slow to become angry, because our anger does not produce the righteousness that God desires."*
>
> —James 1:19-20

Most of us, if we are honest, will admit that more of our angry episodes are cases of unholy wrath than of righteous indignation. Although our emotion often prevents us from seeing it while we are still angry, there is a difference between good and bad anger. How can we explain that difference?

As with most of the sins we're discussing, anger can go wrong in two main ways. First, our anger can have the *wrong object*. In these instances, what we are angry about is inappropriate. Our anger has the wrong target.

Sometimes what makes us angry is the result of a misperception or misunderstanding—there is no real offense; only an imagined one. Or it's one of those "don't kill the messenger" situations where we lash out at the nearest available person since we can't reach or find the true offender. (See Genesis 3 for an early example of our quickness to blame another for our problems!) Often our high expectations for what we are due trigger anger. So it's worth noticing the patterns of recurring anger in our lives. What are we really angry about, and why?

Anger is always ostensibly about justice—getting what we rightly deserve. But anger's power and its potential for destruction are greatest when the injustice hits closest to home; we are angrier when *we* don't get what we deserve than when *others* don't get what they deserve. If it seems that our anger is missing the target, we do well to step back and get a second opinion on whether our anger is truly justified or merely a self-serving rationalization.

The second way our anger can go wrong is in *how we express it*. Here again, we need to pay attention to the patterns of anger in our lives. How angry are you, and how are you expressing your anger? Does your anger make you feel out-of-control or enraged?

If we have a legitimate grievance, but completely lose our cool over it, our anger is excessive—that is, disproportionate to the offense. Or we might get angry too quickly, like the hotheads the writer of Proverbs warns us about. Other times, especially when we suppress anger without dealing with it, our anger lasts too long. When that happens, resentment may eat away at us from the inside and turn slowly into hatred or a sinister plot for revenge.

Worse yet, the two ways anger goes wrong can be combined into one monstrous package: we can be way too angry, or angry way too long, about something or someone we shouldn't be angry with at all.

St. Augustine's Prayer Book (ed. Rev. Loren Gavitt) distinguishes three types of sinful anger: *resentment, pugnacity*, and *retaliation*. Resentful anger includes "dissatisfaction with the abilities and opportunities God has given you ('It's not fair!'), unjustified complaint at the circumstances of your life, . . . blaming God, your parent(s), society, or other individuals for your problems, being judgmental and easily displeased. . . ." Pugnacity, or fighting, includes "attack upon another in anger, murder in deed or desire, nursing grudges, injury to another by striking, cursing, or insulting . . . or by damaging another's reputation or property, being quarrelsome . . ." And retaliation can take the forms of "vengeance for wrongs (real or imagined) or simply plotting revenge, dealing out harsh or excessive punishment, refusal to forgive or to offer or accept reconciliation, . . . shutting others out for selfish reasons, spoiling another's pleasure by uncooperativeness or disdain because you have not gotten your way."

It's good for me to have to type that long list, item by item, just as it is good for you to read it. It is often easy for us to overlook the ways our anger is out of line because our expression of anger may not conform to the usual picture of an angry person yelling at the top of her lungs. But because anger is fueled by our expectations for ourselves and what we are due, any warping of those expectations can lead to recurring patterns of misdirected or excessive anger.

The key to overcoming these sins, as with the other sins, is not just to treat surface symptoms but to recognize their rootedness in a deeper problem.

Think It Over

Go through the list of the three expressions of anger from *St. Augustine's Prayer Book* (above). Mark the expressions of anger you see in yourself. Can you think of others that are not listed? What do you think is the root of your anger?

In Other Words

"Of the Seven Deadly Sins, anger is possibly the most fun. To lick your wounds, to smack your lips over grievances long past, to roll over your tongue the prospect of bitter confrontations still to come, to savor to the last toothsome morsel both the pain you are given and the pain you are giving back—in many ways it is a feast fit for a king. The chief drawback is that what you are wolfing down is yourself. The skeleton at the feast is you."

—Frederick Buechner, *Wishful Thinking*

Live It Out

Keep a journal for a week. Record all the times you get angry. In each instance, identify the object of your anger, and rate how angry you were on a scale from one to five (five being really, really mad!). Leave the journal for a week, and then look back at it. What have you learned?

Selfless or Selfish? 4

"Therefore each of you must put off falsehood and speak truthfully to your neighbor, for we are all members of one body. 'In your anger do not sin': Do not let the sun go down while you are still angry, and do not give the devil a foothold. Those who have been stealing must steal no longer, but must work, doing something useful with their own hands, that they may have something to share with those in need. Do not let any unwholesome talk come out of your mouths, but only what is helpful for building others up according to their needs, that it may benefit those who listen. And do not grieve the Holy Spirit of God, with whom you were sealed for the day of redemption. Get rid of all bitterness, rage and anger, brawling and slander, along with every form of malice. Be kind and compassionate to one another, forgiving each other, just as in Christ God forgave you."

—Ephesians 4:25-32

In my collection of seven deadly sins paraphernalia, I have a book called *Divinely Decadent*, which depicts "a lavish collection of wicked home interiors," arranged according to the seven vices they represent. One of the pictures for the sin of wrath is a giant crystal chandelier lying smashed in a heap with a crystal-handled steel knife plunged into the middle of the pile. The authors describe it as an "unsettling still life." Wrath may be a common sin, but its intentions, as this arresting image shows us, are ultimately chilling.

The film *The Mission* tells about the work of the Jesuits among South American Indian tribes in the eighteenth century. It includes two scenes that vividly contrast anger's life-threatening and life-giving effects. In the first scene, Rodrigo (played by Robert DeNiro) is a slave trader who returns to the city to discover that his lover has fallen for his brother instead. When he comes upon the two of them in bed together, he storms out in furious silence. His brother runs after him, pleading for understanding, but the two quickly come to blows. After a brief swordfight, Rodrigo stabs his brother and then stands over him, watching him bleed to death. His anger was impulsive, excessive, and had a deadly effect. He feels terrible remorse for his brother's murder.

Later Rodrigo repents and becomes a priest, accompanying Father Gabriel (Jeremy Irons) to a mission in a remote Indian village. The villagers come to accept the priests and Christianity. When the villagers are threatened by white men practicing the slave trade, Rodrigo, still a man of the sword at heart, feels the need to defend them against the military might of those who would destroy the mission and take away its people. Gabriel knows that their role as priests denies them this option (Catholic priests are forbidden to take up arms and shed blood because they represent Christ).

Rodrigo comes into Father Gabriel's room at the mission to tell him that he wants to renounce his vows of obedience and fight—

and not only him, but the other priests too. Father Gabriel, ordinarily an imperturbable and gentle man, becomes angry with him. The way of the world is violence, he vehemently tells Rodrigo. "You made a vow to God, and *God is love*!"

> **Word Alert**
>
> In some Christian traditions, men and women who joined a religious community would take a voluntary *vow of obedience*, imitating the obedience of Christ.

Whichever side we take, this interchange is instructive about anger. In this case, Gabriel's anger is motivated not by personal gain or by what he thinks is his due. It is motivated by what he thinks *God* is due, and by the spiritual good of the villagers and of Rodrigo. His anger expresses his desire to live according to love, not violence. And his chastisement is not meant to inflame Rodrigo but to instruct him in the ways of love and persuade him to be faithful to his vows. The film ends with Rodrigo laying down his life fighting for the Indian villagers, and Gabriel leaving the village church to offer the communion bread to his enemies. Both die in their attempts to show love and defend justice.

The contrast between the two scenes illustrates the differences between the "what" and the "how" of sinful wrath and righteous anger. In the conflict with his brother, Rodrigo's desire is self-centered—he wants this woman for himself, and his brother has taken her away. His manner of expressing his anger led to murder. Father Gabriel, by contrast, shows us anger in the service of love and justice—anger in the service of God and the good of his neighbor. Gabriel's manner of expressing his anger to Rodrigo led to a disagreement between them, but a respectful one that harmed neither.

Anger can be holy or harmful, selfless or selfish. What form does it take in your life?

Think It Over

Brainstorm a list of angry episodes, either real or fictional (from books, TV, or movies), and try to figure out in each instance *what* the person was angry about and *how* he or she expressed anger. Analyze the examples together—are these examples of anger serving love and justice, or are they examples of sinful and selfish wrath?

In Other Words

"Not forgiving is like eating rat poison and then waiting for the rat to die."

—Anne Lamott, *Traveling Mercies*

Live It Out

Watch the two film clips from *The Mission* discussed above (chapter 8, "A Brother's Death" and chapter 22, "Sword in Hand"). Better yet, watch the whole film.

Slow to Anger 5

*"The LORD is compassionate and gracious,
slow to anger, abounding in love."*
—Psalm 103:8

When I first started researching anger and the sin of wrath,
I checked my study Bible's concordance for Scriptural references
to anger. I expected most of the Old Testament references to
describe the stereotypical God of wrath. Instead I was surprised to
find a constant refrain that is repeated in book after book, almost
word for word: "The LORD is merciful and gracious, slow to anger
and abounding in steadfast love." Any reader of the Old Testament wouldn't make it through two books without being hit over
the head with that recurring theme.

When I teach about the vice of anger to my students, I have them
look up all the passages, one after the other. Exodus, Numbers,
Nehemiah, Psalms, Jonah. . . . By the eighth one or so, they start
to get the point! Do we?

There are some ways that our anger should *not* be like God's—
after all, we are not responsible for securing justice for the entire
universe. In fact, it is usually when we assume it is (and then take
on ourselves God's role in doling out retribution), that our anger
blows past its rightful bounds. But there are other important

ways our anger *should* be like God's, and this is the main one: we should be slow to anger and abounding in steadfast love.

Proverbs is full of warnings against anger. Most of them are about hotheads, as in the verse we quoted on day 3 of this week's readings. We get angry too quickly, according to Proverbs 14:16-17; 17:27; 22:24-25; 29:11, 22 (to take a sample), and would do better to cool down and hold back. We storm around and fly off the handle and blow our tops, but God is slow to anger. How can we learn to be more like God?

Dealing with anger requires that we understand ourselves as a union of mind and body. Anger is often a matter of setting realistic expectations, of making room for more flexibility in what we require of ourselves and others, of regaining perspective and making sure we have not over-inflated our claims on the world.

Anger—the emotion designed to make us sensitive to injustice in relationships between people—often puts blinders on us. Instead of seeing the claims of others, our anger narrows our focus only to what we claim as our due. Humor is a great way to stave off anger and tame it when it flares. Humor gives us perspective and helps us take ourselves a little less seriously. Being able to laugh at ourselves counters our tendency to indulge our emotions and stoke them by "replaying the tapes" in our minds, which further distorts our perspective on what really happened.

However, managing anger is also a matter of giving our bodies what they need. These needs include getting enough rest and exercise, having enough space, and enjoying fulfilling relationships. Listening to music, receiving a soothing touch, or going for a walk are all physical ways to burn off the tension and toxins that build up from recurrent stressors in our lives and help us be "slow to anger" and quicker to dissipate our anger.

Finally, we can discipline ourselves by taking a time-out from the situation that triggers our anger. That means physically removing ourselves from the situation for a while (or at least distracting ourselves with something else) until we can turn back to deal with the problem calmly and with perspective.

Ultimately, though, these action strategies for overcoming a habit of anger must change our heart and vision. Dealing with anger requires getting to its root. Who am I? What gives me a secure place from which to live, and what makes me feel threatened? Can I really trust God to handle things? Why are my claims on the world so demanding, and why are they so rarely met?

When anger turns destructive, it usually expresses a desire to reassert our power over a situation or person, when what we really feel is a total lack of control. Anger is rooted in pride. To overcome it, we need to learn, and relearn, and relearn again, our confidence in God's justice and his control over our lives.

Think It Over

1. What are your anger triggers? What do they tell you about your expectations for yourself and your life?

2. What strategies work best to help you overcome destructive anger?

In Other Words

"Beloved, never avenge yourselves, but leave room for the wrath of God; for it is written, 'Vengeance is mine, I will repay, says the Lord.'"

—Romans 12:19

Live It Out

Use the Desert Fathers' strategy for countering temptation: memorize a verse of Scripture that counters your tendencies to anger and repeat it slowly to yourself when you find yourself in a situation that sparks your temper. (This practice follows Jesus' example in his desert temptations to use the Word against the devil's temptations.)

Wrath
Discussion Guide

Anger can be a problematic subject in the Christian tradition. Most people will admit that, in principle, anger can be good if rightly directed (at injustice or at our own sin). The problem is that anger so quickly and so easily spins out of control and becomes self-serving and harmful.

Anger at its best is rooted in a desire for justice and formed by love for everyone in the situation. At its worst, anger is directed at those who don't deserve it and is expressed in disproportionate and destructive ways. There are different ways to show our anger: some people are hotheads, others resentful or vindictive. Most often our own unrealistic or self-centered expectations trigger our anger.

When taking off our old, sinful practices and clothing ourselves with Christ, we need to look at what makes God angry, and how God gets angry. There's a recurring refrain in Scripture that gives us a model to follow: God is "slow to anger and abounding in steadfast love." Like God's anger, ours should be rooted in love for others and not quickly aroused.

For Starters
(10 minutes)

Warmly welcome anyone who is new to your group. Be sure to "bring them up to speed" by briefly summarizing your last session. The review won't hurt the rest of you either.

Little things often make us angry. A family member accidentally deletes a key file on your computer; your spouse leaves his or her dirty socks in the living room; a telemarketer interrupts your supper. . . . Invite group members to share something that made them angry this past week and then reflect on how irritation over small issues can lead to more serious forms of anger.

Or, invite group members to share one insight from the daily devotions that was meaningful for them. Don't discuss it now, just mention it.

Let's Focus
(5 minutes)

Review the introduction to this session, and then have someone read this focus statement aloud:

The sin of wrath emerges when certain patterns of anger get entrenched in our minds, hearts, and actions. Most often, a narrowly selfish outlook or an exaggerated sense of what we deserve is at the root of wrath. Love can motivate both gentleness and anger, as Christ and many Christians show us by their example. God's anger is rooted in his "steadfast love" and the desire for justice—not only for himself but for others. To become more like Christ, our anger must be rightly directed and fittingly expressed.

Word Search
(20 minutes)

Discuss the following Scripture passages (or, if you're running short on time, choose the ones the group wants to discuss):

*   John 2:13-17

    How does Jesus display anger here?

    What is he angry about?

    We know Jesus is sinless, but how do you explain and justify his anger here?

- Proverbs 17:27; Ephesians 4: 26-27; James 1:19-20
  What advice do these passages offer us in dealing with anger?

  Which one do you find especially helpful?

- Amos 2:6-8
  What is the cause of God's wrath here?

  What does it tell us about when our anger is justified or even necessary? (Don't forget that the most common expression in the Bible about God's anger is that he is "*slow* to anger.")

Bring It Home
(20 minutes, or as time allows)

Choose *one* of the following options.

Option 1
On your board or a sheet of newsprint, **jot down examples of anger that group members recall from their own experience.** Then discuss which examples are cases of holy anger (and why) and which ones are not by looking at both *what* the person was angry about and *how* the anger was expressed. Are there cases in which Christians should be *more* angry than they are?

Option 2
As time permits, choose among the following questions and discuss them:

- Describe an admirable, constructive expression of anger that you have seen or experienced. How can the emotion of anger be channeled into good actions?

- Some people seem to have a greater struggle with anger than others. Why might this be? (Reflect on the root causes of anger.)

- All of us get angry at times. Describe some ways that help you resist letting your anger get the upper hand. *Hint:* One of the most helpful things we can do when we feel angry with somebody is admit it and take responsibility for it—"I feel angry because . . ."

Option 3

Have two volunteers act out a scene in which a husband (or wife) comes home late from work for the fourth day in a row (without calling his or her spouse). Run the scene as many ways as you can imagine, according to the spouse's various expressions of anger. Which of these angry responses are humorous? Which ones are dangerous? Are any constructive? Why?

Pray It Through

(10 minutes)

Take time to suggest items to pray about together.

In your prayer together, also ask God for some or all of the following:

- That we not become blinded by anger
- That our anger be rooted in love
- That our anger be caused by genuine injustice and not mere selfish interests
- That our anger be expressed in ways that build up and call to account, rather than tear down or destroy
- That our anger be tempered by gentleness and humility
- That our sense of justice be keen enough to move us to action on others' behalf and overcome our indifference or apathy

Live It Out

(Each day during the coming week)

Godliness is being like God. At two set times throughout the day pray that God will help you be "slow to anger" and "abounding in love," so that this refrain becomes ingrained in your heart and mind.

> **Web Alert**
>
> **Be sure to check out the participants' section for this session on www.GrowDisciples.org for interesting links and suggestions for readings and activities that will deepen your understanding of the sin of anger.**

To forgive is to give up the right to hurt someone else.

Is it true, is it kind, is it necessary??

Session 4
Gluttony

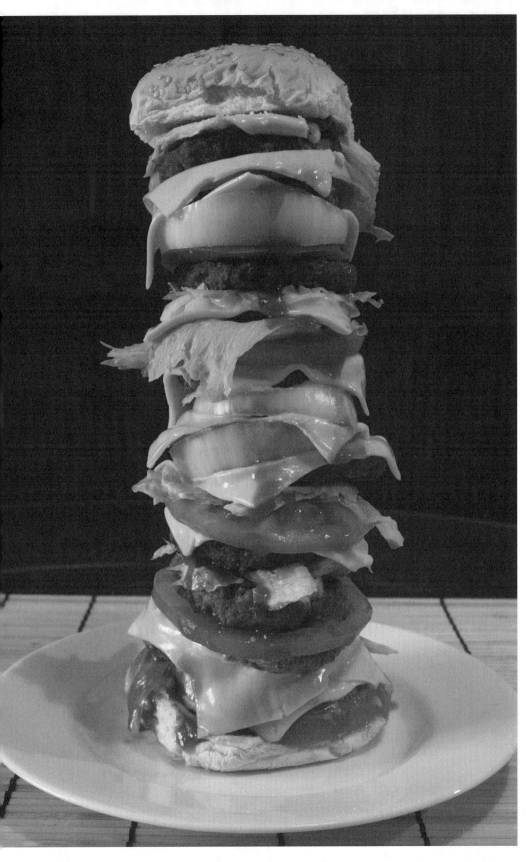

A Selfish Obsession 1

"'I have the right to do anything' you say—but not everything is beneficial. 'I have the right to do anything'—but I will not be mastered by anything."

—1 Corinthians 6:12

In the late eighties, *Harper's Magazine* ran a series of spoof advertisements on the seven deadly sins called "You Can Have It All." The ad shows an enormously obese person leaping blissfully into a pool of water, while a crowd of spectators watches with mouths agape, like the audience at SeaWorld—making the comparison of the leaping man to a whale irresistible. The caption reads *The Glutton Society: Helping People Make the Most of Themselves for Over 100 Years.*

> **Word Alert**
>
> In case you've never been there, *SeaWorld*'s thrilling shows feature killer whales and other marine mammals working with their human trainers to perform leaps and flips in a large pool of water.

People who are overweight are the targets of relentless and vicious ridicule and castigation. Do they have to shoulder the additional burden of being labeled gluttons?

The first thing we need to do when studying the sin of gluttony is to identify what it is *not*. Gluttony is *not* defined as being over—

even way over—one's ideal or healthy weight (nor is that a sin). Nor is it defined as overeating.

Overly thin people may also struggle with food, sometimes developing conditions like anorexia or bulimia.

> **Word Alert**
>
> *Anorexia* and *bulimia* are increasingly common eating disorders in our society that worships thinness. Anorexics, rather than giving into the pleasures of eating, seek control over their bodies (and their lives) by avoiding food.

What then is the sin of gluttony? It is allowing our desire for the pleasures of food and eating to dominate us. What's wrong with gluttons is that they are "mastered" by it.

Food tastes good, and so when we eat it we get both the pleasure of tasting it and the pleasure of feeling full. God created food, and God commanded Adam and Eve to eat in the garden. Clearly there is nothing unlawful about eating in and of itself, and no foods that are intrinsically bad.

So how much is too much? This is the wrong question (or at best a secondary issue). How much are you captive to the pleasure of eating? That is the first and fundamental question for scouting out gluttony. How painful would it be to live without that pleasure? How life-disrupting would it be to experience a vacuum where that pleasure used to be?

I once voluntarily gave up all snacking for several weeks in a row. I was shocked and dismayed at how difficult I found it. Not only did I miss some of my favorite snacks (I learned that celery is not a satisfying substitute for cookies or chips!), but I also came to realize just how much I looked forward to certain parts of my day because there would be food. The whole day's expectations, small perks, and moments of consolation were built on the pleasures I associated with eating. I suddenly felt "dominated" by something I had been sure I could easily do without. I didn't realize the hold those desires for the pleasure of eating had on me.

Imagine how hard it would be for you to give up—for a week (or a month!)—all sweets (or coffee, or soda, or snacks). Notice that none of these things are necessary for life or health. They're "luxury" foods—things we eat or drink just because we like them.

Why are you eating? What are you eating for? Eating food is pleasurable, as is drinking. And pleasure is good. But pleasure can also become a god that masters us and eventually ruins our ability to appreciate the food we eat, the people we eat it with, and the God who provides it. When that happens, gluttony is the problem.

Think It Over

1. What are some of your stereotypes about gluttony? Do they make you feel guiltier or did they serve to make gluttony the problem "other people" had?

2. Have you ever felt the force of excessive pleasure-seeking in this area? Do you think of yourself as "typical glutton"? Is there such a thing?

In Other Words

"Virtuous people avail themselves of the things of this life with the moderation of a user, not the attachment of a lover."

—St. Augustine

Live It Out

Instead of imagining what it might be like, try the experiment described above. Ask yourself, What would be the hardest thing to give up, *and why*? Then actually try to give it up for a week or a month. After the experiment, reflect on your experience. Were you right about how the level of struggle you experienced? When did you feel most tempted? What does this say about the place of pleasure in your life?

F.R.E.S.H. 2

"Join together in following my example, brothers and sisters, and just as you have us as a model, keep your eyes on those who live as we do. For, as I have often told you before and now tell you again even with tears, many live as enemies of the cross of Christ. Their destiny is destruction, their god is their stomach, and their glory is in their shame. Their mind is set on earthly things. But our citizenship is in heaven. And we eagerly await a Savior from there, the Lord Jesus Christ, who, by the power that enables him to bring everything under his control, will transform our lowly bodies so that they will be like his glorious body."

—Philippians 3:17-21

In the sixth century, Pope Gregory the Great inspired a little ditty for gluttony. It goes like this: "Hastily, sumptuously, excessively, greedily, daintily." With or without a catchy tune, this medieval verse is a helpful reminder of the five forms gluttony can take. As we saw in yesterday's daily reading, it is all too easy for us to reduce the vice of gluttony to the act of overeating. To do so is to miss gluttony's distinctive feature—the selfish obsession with the pleasure of eating. But to oversimplify gluttony as overeating also misses four other forms of this vice, some subtle enough they may even show up in our own eating habits!

In his satire *The Screwtape Letters*, C. S. Lewis has one devil boast to another how he has successfully hoodwinked human beings into thinking they no longer have a gluttony problem, when really what they have done is switched forms—from the "gluttony of excess" to the "gluttony of delicacy."

Perhaps a more memorable acronym for Gregory's list is F.R.E.S.H.: that is, eating too fussily, ravenously, excessively, sumptuously, and hastily. Two of these—fussily and sumptuously—are forms of gluttony that focus on what we eat, and why. Let's take a look at what these forms of gluttony are like.

Eating too fussily is not merely a matter of liking certain foods and disliking others, or even having a discriminating palate. Rather, it is caring too much about the way food is prepared and wanting it to be prepared "just the way I like it" or I won't be satisfied.

In *The Screwtape Letters*, C. S. Lewis describes a woman with this sort of gluttony: "She is always turning away from what has been offered to her to say with a demure little sigh and a smile 'Oh please, please . . . all I want is a cup of tea, weak but not too weak, and the teeniest weeniest bit of really crisp toast.' . . . She never recognises as gluttony her determination to get what she wants, however troublesome it may be to others. . . . The woman is in what may be called the 'All-I-want' state of mind."

The second type of what-we-eat gluttony is eating "too sumptuously." In this form of gluttony, our pleasure-seeking is excessively tuned to the foods that offer the most satiety, or feeling of fullness. In short, this is why low carb/high fat diets work. You get to eat foods that satisfy. This is also why the American diet is full of beef, butter, and cream sauces. They taste rich and filling, and they are. The need to restrain and retrain the desires to eat "too sumptuously" (among other reasons) shapes Lenten fasting for many Christians from centuries past to today: during Lent, they give up "sumptuous" foods—meat and dairy products—and eat only vegetables and bread. Is our diet so saturated with sumptuous food that we can no longer even understand what a life without them would look like?

Word Alert

The purpose of fasting and prayer during *Lent* (the forty weekdays before Easter) is to prepare believers to commemorate the events of Holy Week. These events culminate in the Easter celebration of the resurrection.

As William Ian Miller once pointed out, if it were enough just to enjoy the taste of the foods we like, and then spit them out, dieting would be easy. Gluttony is not only about the pleasure of taste, but also the pleasure of being full, and filling ourselves. The glutton consumes for the sake of pleasure, whether consuming a little or a lot. The first two forms of gluttony—the gluttony of delicacy and sumptuousness—often fly under our radar. Once we learn their names, we can begin to see how much selfish pleasure-seeking drives our own eating in these ways.

Think It Over

1. Look at the story of the Israelites' grumbling for meat in Exodus 16. Notice that they ask for quail after God has already given them manna. Does this episode qualify as an example of "too sumptuous" gluttony?

2. Can you think of a similar example in your own life? Once they got the quail, do you think the Israelites were content? Would you be? What does that teach you about the human appetite?

In Other Words

"But godliness with contentment is great gain. For we brought nothing into the world, and we can take nothing out of it. But if we have food and clothing, we will be content with that."

—1 Timothy 6:6-8

Live It Out

For a week, write down what you eat each day in a food journal. At the end of the week, look it over again. How much of what you ate was driven by your desire for pleasure and satisfaction? Are any of the foods you listed "fussy" or "sumptuous" foods for you?

Sneaky Snacking 3

"When the apostles returned, they reported to Jesus what they had done. Then he took them with him and they withdrew by themselves to a town called Bethsaida, but the crowds learned about it and followed him. He welcomed them and spoke to them about the kingdom of God, and healed those who needed healing. Late in the afternoon the Twelve came to him and said, 'Send the crowd away so they can go to the surrounding villages and countryside and find food and lodging, because we are in a remote place here.' He replied, 'You give them something to eat.' They answered, 'We have only five loaves of bread and two fish—unless we go and buy food for all this crowd.' (About five thousand men were there.) But he said to his disciples, 'Have them sit down in groups of about fifty each.' The disciples did so, and everyone sat down. Taking the five loaves and the two fish and looking up to heaven, he gave thanks and broke them. Then he gave them to the disciples to set before the people. They all ate and were satisfied, and the disciples picked up twelve basketfuls of broken pieces that were left over."

—Luke 9:10-17

The last three forms of gluttony are perhaps more familiar to us: *hastily* (too soon), *greedily*, and *excessively* (too much). Eating too hastily can including sneaking food before the appointed hour of eating, as well as inhaling one's food too quickly. Sneaky snacking is likely just as much a contemporary phenomenon as it was in the medieval monastery!

Eating greedily means gobbling food quickly to make sure you are getting all that you want without having to share or curb your desires. If you had siblings growing up, you know how this works: you have to chow down the first helping faster than anyone else so that you can grab the last piece of pizza in the box before anyone else does. The greedy eater eyes everyone else as they are served: Who got the most? He is not as much concerned with eating more as he is with eating more than everyone else.

Finally, the excessive eater is so dominated by the desire for pleasure that she will keep on eating past the point of fullness. "Just one more piece . . . mmmm, it tastes so good." The promise of more pleasure overrides our awareness of need, of healthful balance, or concern for social grace.

Sometimes these forms all go together. My children have invented the term "shoveling" to sum up the way eating looks when it is too hasty, too greedy, and excessive all at once. Gluttony is an insatiable god, for our taste for pleasure never seems to slake. "All human toil is for the mouth, yet the appetite is never satisfied," writes the author of Ecclesiastes.

There is something a little pathetic about the sin of gluttony, especially in these last three forms. Picture it: human beings—the crown of creation, created for spiritual fellowship with God and others, able to write symphonies and perform brain surgery—sitting with two elbows on the table, shoveling in food as if we'll never get enough. *And we can't.* That's what makes gluttony—or any kind of physical pleasure-seeking—so insatiable and so addictive. We can't fill ourselves with food. We can't be satisfied with pleasure alone.

John Cassian, a Christian theologian celebrated in both the Western and Eastern churches for his spiritual writings, once compared the seven deadly sins to the seven tribes of Canaan that the Israelites were commanded to destroy. Gluttony, however, he compared instead to Egypt—the nation left behind but not destroyed. We need to eat, he said, and while we have bodies that need food, we will never escape the temptation to misuse food altogether.

We might find the ascetic practices of Cassian and the other Desert Fathers somewhat shocking: they slept only four hours a night (on the ground), dressed in rags, ate only bread, a few vegetables, and water—and not to the point of fullness. Their writings often seem to imply that having bodies that need food at all is a bad thing. (On the other hand, they did leave their desert solitude once a week to gather for worship and a shared meal, and would leave their prayers at other times to provide food and hospitality to a guest.)

Perhaps it is a good balance in favor of affirming the goodness of creation that we do not regularly engage in the same ascetic disciplines today. But it might be worth asking ourselves whether these earlier Christians might be equally shocked at our eating habits, our habitually excessive consumption, our pleasure-centered lives that demand immediate gratification. They not only *prayed*, "Give us today our daily bread"; they *lived* it.

You and I are probably more enslaved to the pleasure of eating than we realize. Could we blend into that crowd of five thousand

and hear Jesus thank God for the food, bless it and break it, eat our fill, and realize we have twelve basketsful left over?

Think It Over

1. How do our cultural practices (eating alone, eating in front of the TV or in the car, eating quickly to get to evening events) shape our eating habits? How do these eating habits in turn shape our desires for and attitudes toward food?

2. Consider the widespread practice of dieting. Are diets effective against gluttony? Why or why not?

In Other Words

"A glutton is one who raids the icebox for a cure for spiritual malnutrition."

—Frederick Buechner, *Wishful Thinking*

Live It Out

Take a look at your food journal (see yesterday's "Live It Out"). This time, keep track of the times you ate too hastily, greedily, or excessively. See if you can correlate these kinds of eating with your spiritual or emotional state at the time.

Meal Ready to Eat 4

"They devoted themselves to the apostles' teaching and to fellowship, to the breaking of bread and to prayer. Everyone was filled with awe at the many wonders and signs performed by the apostles. All the believers were together and had everything in common. They sold property and possessions to give to anyone who had need. Every day they continued to meet together in the temple courts. They broke bread in their homes and ate together with glad and sincere hearts, praising God and enjoying the favor of all the people. And the Lord added to their number daily those who were being saved."

—Acts 2:42-47

For the last few years now, the United States has been fighting a war in Iraq. I have watched several students and a family member serving in the Marine Corps be deployed overseas for months at a time. One of those students introduced me to the MRE—an acronym for "Meal Ready to Eat." He ate an MRE almost every day for eight months in a row when he was on active duty.

MREs are individual meals encased in a lightweight waterproof package. They're designed to withstand being dropped (without a parachute) by helicopter 100 feet to troops on the ground. With a parachute, MREs can be dropped from about 1,200 feet. They can survive temperature extremes from minus-60 to 120 degrees Fahrenheit and have a minimum shelf life of three years; some have lasted for decades. After meeting those requirements, you'd expect them to be pretty tasty, right? Sure.

The meals—while not exactly gourmet fare—are designed to supply enough energy and nourishment to sustain soldiers on a mission. They typically contain a main entrée, crackers and cheese or peanut butter and jelly spread, a dessert or snack (the pound cake isn't bad), a beverage packet, and accessories (plastic silverware, napkin, salt and pepper, and a tiny bottle of Tabasco sauce—which the Marines report they put on almost every entrée). They are also equipped with a "flameless ration heater," a packet that, when combined with water, will chemically heat the MRE entrée without any fire or cooking tools, which might give away the troops' position or be too cumbersome to haul. The inclusion of dessert and spices even in MREs indicates that eating, even in dire circumstances, is not best reduced to a mere necessity.

Serving as a Marine involves daily discipline. Eating, sleeping, and other daily activities are all shaped by the mission and what it requires. Marines are responsible to carry out their assigned duties; their own pleasure is subordinate to that goal. Clearly soldiers need food, but if their eating turns gluttonous, it will impact their whole unit and its ability to carry out its mission.

Now contrast the life of a Marine in the field with a glutton's way of life. Gluttons eat first for their own pleasure. Their personal gratification *is* the goal. They structure the rest of their lives and priorities around it, and they subordinate the good of others (or even their own good) to it. North Americans often act as if eating were a private act with no social consequences. This seems false. Like Marines, Christians have a corporate mission that requires individual, daily discipline.

This mission—whether military or religious—can also be *celebrated* through a shared meal. Someone I knew in Iraq sent back a picture of a group of Marines standing in front of a huge cake with gaudy pink icing that spelled out, "Happy Birthday, Marine Corps." Given that temperatures regularly topped 100 degrees at their base, they probably had to eat that cake quickly before the frosting melted! The point is, even the Marines stopped long enough to eat food together that reminded them of their shared identity and mission. Their operations needed to be fed not only by basic nourishment, but also by a sense of who they were and why they were there. Their eating together confirmed and symbolized that *who they are* is a corporate identity, and *what they do* is a corporate mission.

Christians too need food for basic physical nourishment. But we also eat tasty, well-prepared meals as signs of God's goodness. Food is a gift to be enjoyed. It's no accident that Christians are called regularly to eat together as they gather for worship. This meal, the Lord's Supper, feeds us spiritually and confirms our common membership in Christ's body, the church. It's even better when this sacramental meal spills over into a hearty potluck in the fellowship hall.

"You are what you eat" is a slogan not just to scare dieters away from temptation, but a reminder of the importance of what and why we eat together as Christians.

Think It Over

Read Matthew 26:17-30; Mark 14:12-26; and Luke 22:7-23, and reflect on the Lord's Supper. Why do you think the main sacrament of the church is a feast that centers on eating and drinking?

In Other Words

"The flesh when restrained more than is right is often weakened even for the performance of good deeds, so that while hastening to stifle the forces of sin within, it does not have enough strength to pray or preach. And so while pursuing the enemy, we slay the citizen we love."

—Gregory the Great, *Moralia* XXX.18

Live It Out

Consider buying some MREs (available online or at Army surplus stores) and eating them. Or share a simple meal that reminds you of your identity as Christians.

Fasting 5

"Then the word of the LORD came to [Elijah]: 'Go at once to Zarephath in the region of Sidon and stay there. I have directed a widow there to supply you with food.' So he went to Zarephath. When he came to the town gate, a widow was there gathering sticks. He called to her and asked, 'Would you bring me a little water in a jar so I may have a drink?' As she was going to get it, he called, 'And bring me, please, a piece of bread.' 'As surely as the LORD your God lives,' she replied, 'I don't have any bread—only a handful of flour in a jar and a little olive oil in a jug. I am gathering a few sticks to take home and make a meal for myself and my son, that we may eat it— and die.' Elijah said to her, 'Don't be afraid. Go home and do as you have said. But first make a small loaf of bread for me from what you have and bring it to me, and then make something for yourself and your son. For this is what the LORD, the God of Israel, says: "The jar of flour will not be used up and the jug of oil will not run dry until the day the LORD sends rain on the land."' She went away and did as Elijah had told her. So there was food every day for Elijah and for the *woman and her family. For the jar of flour was not used up and the jug of oil did not run dry, in keeping with the word of the LORD spoken by Elijah."*

—1 Kings 17:8-16

If you read all of 1 Kings 17, you'll find three stories about how the Lord provides for the people who trust in him. First, God sends ravens to feed Elijah at the Kerith Ravine, east of the Jordan, and he drinks from the water that remains in the brook. Then the brook runs dry. But God's provision does not. Next, God directs Elijah to the town of Zarephath, where the widow trusts God's promise to provide food for her and her son. Later on, when her son dies, the widow cries out to Elijah, and he cries out to the Lord. They have learned to trust God for daily bread, the bread that sustains their lives. Can they learn to trust him in this life-and-death crisis too?

Gluttony is one of the seven deadly sins, which means that it is a habit rooted in pride, the root from which other sins grow. We have noted so far this week that gluttony has more to do with an excessive desire for pleasure than with eating certain foods or in certain quantities. Gluttons make this pleasure—instead of the God who created it—the god and guide for life.

But because food is such a powerful symbol, getting our desires for food twisted also twists our relationships with God and others. Food is a symbol of life, and eating a symbol of having ample provision for life. Food has everything to do with self-preservation.

Food is also a symbol of our social bonds with each other. When someone we love dies, friends and family bring food. When there is a celebration, we feast together. (Think of Jesus' first miracle at Cana.) When guests arrive, we show hospitality by providing a meal. As the saying goes, "Food is love." Eating nourishes our bodies, but it also nourishes us socially and emotionally.

The serious glutton makes pleasure her god, but it is also important to her to be able to provide this pleasure *for herself* (or at least pretend she is independent of God's provision in doing so). Rather than depending on God for life and love, she tries to create a world in which she can get *what* she wants for herself *whenever* the desire arises. Food is a good prop for this game we play because it is something we readily assume we can get for ourselves.

The practice of fasting, done rightly, can keep our desire for pleasure within healthy bounds. It also reminds us—through our physical experience of hunger—that we are needy and dependent creatures. Thus it also promotes a sense of solidarity with others in need. Let's look at these in turn.

Fasting is a practice in which we do without the food we would normally eat. The practice varies widely among Christians today, but according

> **Web Alert**
> Check www.GrowDisciples.org for more on the practice of fasting.

to Aquinas, it should be restrictive enough to "bridle" our desires for pleasure, while still providing for our physical needs. In medieval practice, fasting restricted the number of times of day you would eat (once), the quantity of food (less than would make you feel full), and the kinds of food eaten (meat and dairy were limited).

Fasting is like tithing—a regular practice to check our ever-increasing desires, which, Aquinas says, "increase in force the more we yield to them." It is a counterpoint to our tendency to slide toward greater and greater pleasure-seeking.

Second, fasting helps us re-learn our dependence on God. We share this condition of dependence with every other creature. We are not gods, and we are not capable of providing

Word Alert

Tithing **is a way for Christians to give back our first fruits to God in thanksgiving and recognition that all of what we have comes from God. A tithe is one-tenth of one's income; it is suggested as a guide for grateful giving.**

all that we need for ourselves. Fasting, then, helps us check our tendency to try to take over God's role and instead trust ourselves to provide for our own satisfaction. It is a way of living out what we profess: that food is a gift we receive from God's hand.

Think It Over

1. The liturgical rhythm of the church year is one of fasting and then feasting, not eating in moderation all the time (Advent fast, Christmas feast; Lenten fast, Easter feast). Why do you think this is so?

2. Fasting was a Christian discipline typically joined to the disciplines of prayer and almsgiving. Why do you think these three disciplines go together?

In Other Words

"Fasting reveals the things that control us."

—Richard Foster, *The Freedom of Simplicity*

Fast for a week (or a season like Lent or Advent). Make sure you do it in the ways described above, skipping a meal a day or a type of food. Reflect on your experience. Do you think fasting is an important part of Christian freedom, or should we submit to certain practices recommended by the church as the whole body of Christ together?

Gluttony
Discussion Guide

You may be surprised to learn that the vice of gluttony is more about your desires than about your weight. Overeating may be one symptom of gluttony (whether it leads to weight gain or not), but the real measure of gluttony is not determined by the bathroom scale but by how dominated we are by the pleasures of eating.

Gluttony's excessive attachment to the pleasures of the palate can come in unexpected forms—not only are eating greedily, hastily, and excessively characteristic signs of gluttony, but so is eating too "sumptuously" (richly) and too "fastidiously" (fussily). When our demand for pleasure leads us to eating habits that place *what we want* over concerns for others with whom we eat and our health, pleasure has become our god.

For Christians, eating food has a special significance. Both disciplines like fasting and celebrations that involve eating (the Lord's Supper in particular) can remind us of who we are. As God's own children, we depend on God but are also able to trust in his provision for us. We don't need to supply our own gratification to meet our needs or make us happy. Instead, we can look to God for our "daily bread."

For Starters
(10 minutes)

Jot down three food items that you would find it hardest to cut out of your daily diet for, say, a month. Share lists with the group, looking for items that appear most often. What, if anything, does the choice of items say about eating habits?

Or, invite group members to share one insight from the daily devotions that was meaningful for them. Don't discuss it now, just mention it.

Let's Focus
(5 minutes)

Review the introduction to this session, and then have someone read this focus statement aloud:

Food is a gift from God that has great social and symbolic significance. Gluttony is a habit of letting our desires for the pleasures of eating go to excess. Our focus on selfish gratification gets in the way of our ability to appreciate food as a gift from God and to be genuinely grateful for it. Fasting is a traditional remedy for gluttony because it helps us re-learn to appreciate the simple pleasures of the table, in their proper place.

Word Search
(20 minutes)

Discuss the following Scripture passages (or, if you're running short on time, choose the ones the group wants to discuss):

*   Exodus 16:4-5, 14-30
    What do the rules of God's gift of manna in the desert teach us about our relationship to food?

*   Matthew 4:1-4
    Why do you think changing stones into *bread* was one of Jesus' temptations, and why did he refuse it?

    How did he refuse it?

    What clues does this episode give us about how gluttony operates in our lives and how we overcome it?

- Acts 2:42-47

   Verse 42 mentions the "breaking of bread" in the context of worship, which means communion. Why do you think eating and drinking are central to Christian worship?

   What are the characteristics of the community meals of verses 46-47?

   How do you think these characteristics and eating in community affect the temptation to gluttony?

Bring It Home
(20 minutes, or as time allows)

Choose one of the following options.

Option 1
Bring in some popular magazines (anything off the rack at the supermarket—*Shape, Family Circle, People, Sports Illustrated, Good House-keeping*, and the like) **and distribute them among the group. Page through them together.** What messages does our culture send about food and our reasons for eating it (or not eating it)? Do these messages encourage gluttony, help us resist it, or are they fairly neutral?

Option 2
As time permits, choose among the following questions and discuss them:

- It's often said that we have an "obesity epidemic" in North America. Do you agree? What do you think are the causes? What does it have to do with gluttony?

- What's the purpose of fasting? How is fasting different from dieting? Have you ever practiced fasting and, if so, what has been your experience?

Since food and eating are God's gifts, what eating practices might make for better enjoyment of these gifts?

Option 3

List the five forms of gluttony (F.R.E.S.H.—eating too fussily, ravenously, excessively, sumptuously, and hastily) on your board or on a sheet of newsprint. Rank the forms according to which ones group members struggle with most, encouraging everyone to offer an example of their number-one form. Brainstorm ways to resist these forms of gluttony together.

Pray It Through
(10 minutes)

Take time to suggest items to pray about together.

Reflecting on your discussion, share things for which you would like to pray in relation to holy eating. Pray about them together. You may wish to end by praying together this seventeenth-century prayer from Anglican Bishop Jeremy Taylor:

"Give me the spirit of temperance and sobriety, . . . as may best enable me to serve thee, but not to make provision for the flesh, to fulfill the lusts thereof: Let me not, as Esau, prefer meat before a blessing; but subdue my appetite, subjecting it to reason and the grace of God, being content with what is moderate, and useful, and easy to be obtained; taking it in due time, receiving it thankfully, making it to minister to my body, that my body may be a good instrument of the soul, and the soul a servant of thy Divine Majesty for ever and ever."

Live It Out
(Each day during the coming week)

Plan to practice some form of fasting this week, perhaps one of the following ways:

- Omit desserts
- Omit one meal for three days of the week.
- Eliminate meat and/or dairy from your diet for a few days or a week.
- Eliminate eating for a whole day (making sure you drink plenty of water and juice).

Accompany your fasting with special time set aside for prayer and almsgiving.

Session 5
Sloth

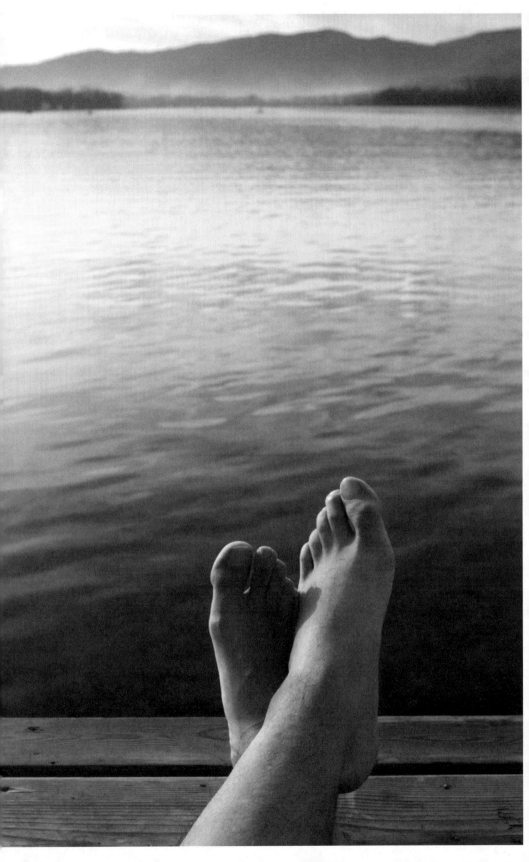

The Noonday Demon 1

"Go to the ant, you sluggard;
consider its ways and be wise!"
—Proverbs 6:6

Of all the deadly sins, sloth is the one that most looks like it does not belong on the list. Sure, it's better to be hard-working than lazy, but since when is being a "sluggard" a sin against God?

> **Word Alert**
>
> A *sluggard* is not a street brawler or a really good hitter in base-ball, but an old word for a lazy person. You might have heard the related word slugabed, a person who stays in bed way too long.

Perhaps the opposite is the case: the caption of *Harper's* spoof advertisement for sloth reads, "If sloth had been the original sin, we'd still be in paradise." And in *The Seven Deadly Sins*, Evelyn Waugh makes a similar case for the "virtue" of slothfulness,

> [Sloth] is a mildly facetious variant of "indolence," and in-dolence, surely, so far from being a deadly sin, is one of the world's most amiable of weaknesses. Most of the world's troubles seem to come from people who are too busy. If only politicians and scientists were lazier, how much hap-pier we should all be. The lazy [person] is preserved from the commission of almost all the nastier crimes.

One could imagine laziness being a bad thing, as when one prefers to veg in front of the TV rather than working to support one's family. But most of the time, laziness amounts to no more than spending an afternoon soaking up the sunshine at the beach, or sitting on the couch watching reruns of *The Office* while munching on a few chips. It's hard to believe that would count as one of the seven deadly sins!

In her self-help parody *Sloth*, Wendy Wasserstein also identifies sloth with a harmless sort of laziness. The book's jacket promises:

> Readers will find out the importance of Lethargiosis—the process of eliminating energy and drive, the vital first step in becoming a sloth. To help you attain the perfect state of indolent bliss, the book offers a wealth of self-help aids. Readers will find the sloth songbook, sloth breakfast bars (packed with sugar, additives, and a delicious touch of Ambien), sloth documentaries (such as the author's 12-hour epic on Thomas Aquinas), and the sloth network, channel 823, programming designed not to stimulate or challenge in any way.

It's not surprising that most people equate sloth with laziness. But it takes a deeper look at the history of sloth to understand what it really is, and why we mostly misunderstand it today.

Sloth's most ancient name is *acedia*. It means "lack of care." Evagrius of Pontus, one of the Desert Fathers, painted this colorful portrait of acedia:

Word Alert

Evagrius of Pontus (A.D. 345-99) was raised in a Christian family. As a young man he was captivated by the delights of Constantinople, the capital of Christianity at the time, becoming a womanizer and a glutton. Coming to his senses, he made his way to Egypt and joined the monks in the desert. His writings were treasured by the early Christians and are widely read yet today.

The demon of acedia, also called the noonday demon . . . is the most oppressive of all the demons. He attacks the monk about the fourth hour [10 a.m.] and besieges the soul until the eighth hour [2 p.m.]. First of all, he makes it appear that the sun moves slowly or not at all, and that the day seems to be fifty hours long. Then he compels the monk to look constantly towards the windows, to jump out of [his desert] cell, to watch the sun to see how far it is from the ninth hour [3 p.m.], to look this way and that. . . . He deploys every device in order to have the mink leave his cell and flee the stadium (*Evagrius of Pontus*, trans. and ed. Robert E. Sinkewicz).

For Evagrius, acedia was weariness and distaste—not just for any work—but for one's calling to a life of Christian discipline. It was extremely serious because it tempted people to bail out from their spiritual identity and vocation. The person afflicted with acedia wants nothing more than to run away from God's claims, God's calling on his or her life. To stay and face them feels like carrying an intolerable weight.

(Word Alert)

Christians believe that they are called to use the gifts God has given them in their *vocation*. This may be in the context of a job to which a person feels called, or in service to others at home, in the neighborhood, or at church outside of our paid employment.

Sloth today usually means the sort of recreational laziness that is no big deal. But Christians have often considered laziness the opposite of diligence, especially diligence that is considered an expression of love or devotion to God. This makes sloth a matter of the heart first.

If our willingness to work is a sign of our devotion to what God wants from us, then resistance or apathy or distaste is a symptom of a lack of devotion—a lack of care. Sloth is not so much laziness, then, as it is laziness about love.

Think It Over

For fun, read the children's book *Revenge of the Sloths* by Helen Lester. How does this story depict sloth? How does this story depict work and its value and purpose? Or find another contemporary example of sloth from books, TV, or movies, and reflect on the questions.

In Other Words

"'It's a lazy afternoon in summer' is a kind of delight, and sloth has no delight. Relaxing is not sloth. The person who never relaxes is not a saint but a fidget."

—Peter Kreeft, *Back to Virtue*

Live It Out

Make a time chart of your day. Did you spend any time being lazy or relaxing? How do you feel about that? Do you feel like a better Christian for being busy and getting a lot accomplished? Is your busyness necessarily a sign of love and devotion, or something else?

The Demands of Love 2

"'Love the Lord your God with all your heart and with all your soul and with all your mind.' You shall love the Lord your God with all your heart, and with all your soul, and with all your mind."

—Matthew 22:37

When I first started teaching sloth, I found it a very puzzling sin. In the tradition, acedia was always classified as a spiritual sin, and a very serious one at that. Thomas Aquinas says it is a sin against love itself. And yet it also had something to do with dejection or oppressiveness, and something to do with effort—this was the laziness link. So how do all these pieces fit together?

Aquinas describes sloth as "sorrow over the divine good in us." Our first response to that that definition is probably, "Huh?" Let's take it piece by piece.

Roughly translated, "the divine good in us" is the Holy Spirit dwelling in our hearts, doing the work of regeneration. So sloth is sorrow over (or aversion to) what the Holy Spirit is doing to make us new.

Why in the world would we be unhappy about that process of transformation? In short, because the Holy Spirit doesn't just conjure our "new selves" out of thin air. The Spirit can't birth a new self unless the old one is put to death. This long, painful process of dying and rising with Christ is called sanctification.

The apostle Paul tells us, "You were taught, with regard to your former way of life, to put off your old self, which is being corrupted by its deceitful desires; to be made new in the attitude of your minds; and to put on the new self, created to be like God in true righteousness and holiness" (Eph. 4:22-24).

Have you ever tried to get rid of an old habit, especially one that gave you some important gratification or psychological prop when you couldn't cope very well? Then you know just what I am talking about when I describe what sloth resists. To "put off your old self" takes effort, perseverance, sacrifice, and change, day after day after day. It's so much easier to stay stuck in our old, familiar sinful ways. It takes effort to let the Holy Spirit create a new heart in us, transform us out of the old mold into the image of Christ.

We can use the analogy of a married couple to help explain how sloth works. The couple has said their vows and committed to loving each other. They *are* married already. Yet *being married* is also a continuing commitment. After their vows, the couple must keep on loving their spouse daily, even if that love requires some daily drudgery, some change of their own personal habits, some sacrifices large and small, some moments when they'd rather sulk or storm off alone after a fight than have the talk that will open the door to forgiveness and reconciliation. In this way, marriage—that is, being married and staying married—is not just "already" but also "not yet." It is a daily, ongoing task. In *The Quotidian Mysteries*, Kathleen Norris says of marriage, "[It's] eternal, but it's also daily, as daily and unromantic as housekeeping."

Our relationship to God is like that—eternal, but daily too. The slothful person wants to claim the love and security of the relationship (that's the easy part!), but not really give herself up daily for the One she loves.

So sloth is resistance to loving God because love asks something of us; it demands that we be transformed. In that sense, it *is* lazy—it prefers the easy way out. Like pop songs and Hollywood romances, this sort of love comes cheap but cannot last. Even if her activities take effort and keep her very busy, the slothful one prefers fantasy, escape, and diversion to facing up to the commitments she has made and what they demand of her.

The slothful person finds accepting God's love oppressive and burdensome; her resistance makes her want to escape or find some easier way. But because we are created to be in relationship with God, we can only find our fulfillment as human beings if we are transformed by love and submit to God's way. That means the slothful person *chooses* her own sorrow—and the familiarity of her old sinful self and way of life—over the joy and fulfillment that comes with accepting the discipline and sacrifice of love.

We often find the ongoing work of love tedious or tiresome, wearying or irritating. Sometimes we would prefer to escape love's daily demands. We can feel oppressed by the tiresomeness of the daily disciplines that bring us closer to God. In sloth, we refuse to accept the truth that love is a commitment, and that we will find joy only through commitment and discipline.

Sloth is sorrowful but stubborn resistance to the demands of love. It refuses the effort of doing what it takes day after day to keep the bonds of love alive. When the going gets tough, the slothful bail out.

Think It Over

In what areas of your life are you most tempted to escape the demands of love? What acts of love do you find a daily burden? What are your favorite diversions or escape strategies?

In Other Words

"The secret is that God loves you exactly the way you are, and that he loves you too much to let you stay that way."

—Anne Lamott, *Traveling Mercies*

Live It Out

Draw a cartoon of a married couple or two long-time friends in a situation where love feels demanding. Does this scenario help in thinking through how sloth looks in your own life? How?

Too Busy? 3

> *"Love so amazing, so divine,*
> *demands my soul, my life, my all."*
>
> —Isaac Watts

> *"Love the Lord your God with all your heart*
> *and with all your soul and with all your*
> *mind and with all your strength."*
>
> —Mark 12:30

My students once gave a presentation on sloth in which they did the time-chart exercise we suggested in the daily reading for day 1 of this week. They showed two charts describing the typical day of two of their college roommates. Roommate 1's chart included the following activities: studying, lab work, sports practice, volunteering, homework, and more homework. Roommate 2's chart included far less: more hanging around with friends, more watching TV, some studying but not as much.

When it came to diligence and avoiding sloth, Roommate 1 came off looking like the big winner. But, my students observed, Roommate 1 kept himself busy all day and never had time for friends or family. When his family called to talk to him, he was usually in the library studying, unavailable to take the call. He was too busy for dates and fun with people in his dorm. When people asked him to hang out, he always had too much homework. He also studied during chapel break and didn't have time for the residence hall Bible study. There was more to his story than first met the eye. What was going on here?

Roommate 1 was using his busyness to avoid relationships—relationships with God and with others. Rather than being a sign of love or devotion, his busyness was a diversion technique he used to avoid loving others. His diligence, in other words, was a mask for something else. Roommate 1, possibly the most industrious student on campus, had a heart full of sloth.

When I first started studying sloth, I was sure that this was one vice I had no problem with. After all, I am hard-working to a fault! But I soon discovered that the danger of measuring sloth by laziness is to overlook the fact that busyness, constant activity, and restlessness are *themselves* classic symptoms of sloth, according to the Christian tradition.

How can this be? When we succumb to the sin of sloth and resist accepting our true identity and our new life in Christ because we are too attached to our old habits and comforts, we are essentially choosing to be unfulfilled. We were made for a relationship of love with God and others, but the slothful person lives in denial of this truth. He must constantly deny his need for love and for God by distracting herself with other things. It is a life of escapism, of fantasy, of never stopping to reflect. Ultimately, when the slothful person recognizes that he cannot live without love's transformation, he falls into despair and is paralyzed by inertia.

Sloth's main symptoms, then, are *restlessness* and *false rest*. The *restless* form of sloth can come in many forms: a life of constant entertainment or social activity, a life of relentless busyness (even at worthwhile or respectable tasks), a life of physical restlessness and spiritual discontentment. In Evelyn Waugh's novel *Brides-head Revisited*, Sebastian Flyte (get it?) moves from one place and project to the next in search of a substitute fulfillment to help him forget about Christ's claims on him. But until he accepts that identity and what it asks of him, he cannot find peace or joy.

We too seek constant diversions when we cannot live in the truth; in fact, we'll do anything but face up to what we are made to be.

Sloth's *false rest* is inertia—the lack of movement and motivation that comes with oppressive sadness, not the relaxed peacefulness of one who is content. Sloth is not to be confused with depression or grief, although it can have similar outer symptoms. Rather it is a matter of the heart and will. It is the condition of feeling "stuck" in a joyless situation that you stubbornly refuse to change because that change will cost you.

Like the married couple who want the joy of marriage and the comfort of unconditional love but are unwilling to forgive each other after a fight, slothful people choose to remain unhappy and to let their relationships with others stagnate. They refuse to let love move them into action. Slothful "rest," then, is procrastination rather than peace.

Think It Over

1. Are you more prone to sloth's restlessness or its false rest? Give examples.

2. What forms of diversion does our culture tempt us to seek? (These forms can involve work *or* recreation *or* even church activities.)

3. What sort of regular practices do you think could help us resist these slothful temptations—from inside and outside the church—together?

In Other Words

"Sloth is not to be confused with laziness. Lazy people, people who sit around and watch the grass grow, may be people at peace. Their sun-drenched, bumblebee dreaming may be the prelude to action or itself an act well worth the acting. Slothful people, on the other hand, may be very busy people. They are people who go through the motions, who fly on automatic pilot. Like somebody with a bad head cold, they have mostly lost their sense of taste and smell. They know something's wrong with them, but not wrong enough to want to do something about it."

—Frederick Buechner, *Wishful Thinking*

Live It Out

Go through your calendar for the week (or a list of your activities that day) with two highlighters in hand. In one color, highlight the activities that arise from your relationships of love with God and others and that continue to feed and nourish those relationships. In another color, highlight the activities that keep you busy but do not nourish your relationship with God or other people. How much of your life are you just staying busy, diverting yourself or avoiding something else you ought to be doing? Choose one of these activities and carve it out of your life for a week.

A Change of Heart 4

"Come to me, all you who are weary and burdened, and I will give you rest. Take my yoke upon you and learn from me, for I am gentle and humble in heart, and you will find rest for your souls. For my yoke is easy and my burden is light."
—Matthew 11:28-30

In the film *Groundhog Day*, big city weatherman Phil Connors gets stuck reliving the same day over and over and over in the small town of Punxatawny, Pennsylvania. Phil takes advantage of his predicament by living a life of flagrant, hedonistic self-gratification. As he scarfs down this third plate of doughnuts, his coworker asks him, "Don't you worry about getting fat? Or cholesterol?" Phil replies, "I don't worry about *anything* anymore."

The main project that keeps him busy, however, is the elaborate seduction of his producer, Rita. Phil is attracted to Rita because of her goodness, but he does not, indeed *cannot*, really love her—at least not yet.

Phil figures out what Rita wants and then puts up just the right false front to manipulate her into giving him what *he* wants from her.

Word Alert

According to tradition, groundhog Punxatawney Phil emerges from his temporary home in Punxatawney on *Groundhog Day*. If Phil sees his shadow and returns to his hole, the country will have six more weeks of winter. If Phil does not see his shadow, spring will arrive early.

Ultimately she sees through Phil's selfish strategy and rejects his advances: "I could never love someone like you, Phil, because you could never love anyone but *yourself!*"

Rita is right. Phil refuses to be open to real love and its demands on him. All his efforts are designed to get what *he* wants, not to offer himself to Rita in love. What Phil doesn't understand is that resisting what he needs to do to be in a genuine relationship of love is to resist his own fulfillment, to choose unhappiness. And that is where we find Phil—in despair.

Sitting apathetically in the Lazy Boy recliner, watching TV, unshowered, unkempt, and drinking himself into oblivion, Phil can no longer hide his unhappiness even from himself. But he still refuses to love.

Both his previous hedonistic diversionary tactics and his subsequent despair and inertia count equally as expressions of sloth. Phil is at an impasse. Sloth naturally gives way to despair.

Finally, however, perhaps out of sheer desperation, Phil attempts to change—to let the demands of love move him from selfishness to selfless giving. He begins, little by little, day after day, to become the sort of person who could be both capable and worthy of love.

This new strategy takes effort. But unlike his previous stratagems, these efforts change Phil's heart.

No longer is Phil bored and restless, filling time with self-centered diversions and empty pleasures. This time he does not merely pretend, but really becomes a person capable of fulfilling the demands of real love.

In the end, Phil finally comes to know real happiness, joy, and peace.

The real work sloth resists, therefore, is not mere physical effort but a change of heart—the kind of change from the old self to the new that love demands of us, the kind of change that makes us capable of genuine love for others in return.

Think It Over

1. Do you sometimes get tired while trying to love?

2. Have you ever experienced a transformation like Phil's, when a relationship came to life because you let love transform your heart and direct your efforts? What was the turning point for you?

In Other Words

"You have made us for yourself, and our hearts are restless until they rest in You."

—Augustine, *Confessions*

Live It Out

Watch *Groundhog Day* (or, if you don't have time, watch these clips: "Perfect Guy" (ch. 17), "Gobbler's Knob" (ch. 18), "Rockmaninoff" (ch. 25), and "A Warm Face" (ch. 27). Compare the old Phil to the new Phil. What do you think made his old life feel so unsatisfying? What makes his new life so satisfying, even though takes just as much effort?

Perseverance 5

"As soon as [the angels] had brought [Lot and his wife and daughters] out [of the city], one of them said, 'Flee for your lives! Don't look back, and don't stop anywhere in the plain! Flee to the mountains or you will be swept away!' But Lot said to them, 'No, my lords, please! Your servant has found favor in your eyes, and you have shown great kindness to me in sparing my life. But I can't flee to the mountains; this disaster will overtake me, and I'll die. Look, here is a town near enough to run to, and it is small. Let me flee to it—it is very small, isn't it? Then my life will be spared.' He said to him, 'Very well, I will grant this request too; I will not overthrow the town you speak of. But flee there quickly, because I cannot do anything until you reach it.' (That is why the town was called Zoar.) By the time Lot reached Zoar, the sun had risen over the land. Then the LORD rained down burning sulfur on Sodom and Gomorrah—from the LORD out of the heavens. Thus he overthrew those cities and the entire plain, destroying all those living in the cities— and also the vegetation in the land. But Lot's wife looked back, and she became a pillar of salt."

—Genesis 19:17-26

This is probably the last passage in Scripture you would have thought of as providing an example of sloth. But it is the one used by the early Christian tradition. Why?

Lot's situation shows a soul that has wandered away from God's call in order to pursue the goods the world offers instead. What Sodom promised looked too good to refuse: the rich plains, the lovely house, the food, the company, the lifestyle. . . . But underneath the attractive veneer that seduces Lot is a life of godlessness and death.

Lot's in deep, but thanks to the pleas of Abraham, God offers to rescue him. The angels plead, they warn, and finally they drag Lot and his family away. But Lot is reluctant to leave behind the substitutes for God to which his heart had

> (Word Alert)
>
> **Archeologists have been looking for the site of *Sodom* for most of the last century. A recent excavation by Steven Collins in Jordan, northeast of the Dead Sea, seems promising. It uncovered the mass destruction of a large city by fire dated around the time of Abraham and Lot.**

grown so attached. He cannot fully accept a life devoted to God, which sounds as dangerous as the mountains to which they try to lead him. Instead he bargains for Zoar . . . away from Sodom, but not too far away—not as far as the mountains to which God wants him to flee.

Lot's wife reveals her heart's true home when she looks back. In the end, she refuses the way out because it will cost her everything—her familiar life, her home, her friends.

It is difficult to strike the right balance when talking about the sort of work and discipline spiritual growth requires of us. We don't want to make the Christian life another legalistic to-do list. But we also don't want to slide into the idea that God doesn't really demand anything of us, and that it won't be painful.

The Desert Fathers said that the only remedy for the sin of sloth is the virtue of perseverance. If the angels had not dragged her forward out of the city, Lot's wife would have slid right back into her old ways. She was unwilling to keep walking forward, away from Sodom. The solution to sloth is to put one foot in front of the other, day after day. Whatever you do, don't run off after something that looks better for a moment. Just keep walking.

In many ways, this is what our daily life as disciples is like. Not every devotional time fills us with joy and inspiration. A friend of mine once criticized others in her church who wanted all the worship services to be more emotionally uplifting. From her perspective, a lot of what we do in worship is like drills in boot camp—we practice and repeat things so many times that when the crises come, our training kicks in without our having to think about it. We may not feel inspired repeating the tasks of worship week after week, but in the end, our worship transforms us.

According to the Desert Fathers, our job is to "cultivate stillness." In a nutshell, this means staying put. It means not running away— whether through industriousness at work or through imaginative diversions at play—from what we're called to be and do. We're called to accept and stay committed to our true spiritual vocation and identity.

Applying the wisdom of the desert today, we can see the spiritual danger of a culture of busy escapism: it too easily and quickly gives us a way out of this disciplined effort of learning to love. Overcoming slothful tendencies requires us to face up to the sources of our own resistance, rather than grasping for a way out or a handy diversion any time we start to feel stretched.

Love flourishes in a context of lasting commitment; sloth flourishes in a context of conveniently easy escape. Which will we choose?

Think It Over

In what areas of your life do you find it hard to "hang in there?" What's at stake; what greater good might be lost if you cut and run? Can you identify your escape mechanisms?

In Other Words

"The spirit of acedia drives the monk out of his cell, but the monk who possesses perseverance will ever cultivate stillness."

—Evagrius of Pontus

Live It Out

Plan a mini-retreat for your day, a time in which you can rest in God's presence. Find a time of quiet and simply be still with the Lord for five or even ten minutes. Notice how this time of "Sabbath rest" impacts the rest of your day.

Many people associate sloth with mere physical laziness, but in the Christian tradition it is always known as a condition of the heart. Sloth is our inner resistance to love, specifically, the love of God which cannot but transform and sanctify us. Becoming more Christlike is a slow process that takes a lifetime; sloth resists the things we need to do to fully participate in that process. Sometimes it is because we don't want to give something up or die to a certain part of ourselves; other times the whole tediousness of the process gets to us, and we are tempted to bail out.

The Desert Fathers called sloth the "most oppressive" of the vices. Because it carries with it a sense of oppressive sorrow (nonclinical depression), many people try to escape the truth about their resistance to God's transforming love, its demands and commitments.

Busyness, workaholism, partying, or restlessness can therefore (and somewhat surprisingly) be symptoms of sloth. Sloth can also show itself as inertia, indifference, lack of engagement, and resentment or even disgust with spiritual things.

Like the other vices, then, sloth shouldn't just be defined by its behavioral symptoms, but as an inner attitude of distaste and resentment for our life in Christ. The slothful seek a comfortable existence because the changes that God's love would make in us seem too difficult to face or too tedious to keep up over the long haul. Slothful people are lazy . . . about their commitments to love and the daily self-sacrifice that love requires.

For Starters
(10 minutes)

On a scale of 1 (not much to do) to 10 (way too busy), how would you rate your daily life? After sharing your ratings discuss whether you generally yearn for more things to do or fewer. Is it hard or easy for you to picture sloth as a problem in your life?

Or, invite group members to share one insight from the daily devotions or the "Living it Out" exercise from last week that was meaningful for them. Don't discuss it now, just mention it.

Let's Focus
(5 minutes)

Review the introduction to this session, and then have someone read this focus statement aloud:

Sloth is laziness and lack of effort, not primarily in the physical sense of the proverbial couch potato, but rather in the sense of not wanting to fully accept and grow in our relationship with God. Slothful people want the Christian life to be more comfortable and convenient, and we resist God when his love demands that we change—especially through daily disciplines that slowly but surely make us into the people God wants us to be.

Word Search
(20 minutes)

Discuss the following Scripture passages (or, if you're running short on time, choose the ones the group wants to discuss):

- Psalm 119:25-32
  In Psalm 119:28 the word *acedia* (sloth) is translated "sorrow." Can you identify with the psalmist?

  Why do you think he struggles with sloth?

Based on the psalm, what sorts of things can one do to overcome sloth?

- Deuteronomy 1:5-8, 19-36
  How is the Israelites' desire to return to the desert slothful?

  How is their pilgrimage to the Promised Land like our spiritual journey?

  What can we learn from their problems and pitfalls along the way about the things that will tempt us to bail out of a life of loving God when the going gets tough?

- Galatians 6:7-10
  How might being "weary in doing good" be related to sloth?

  Have you felt that weariness? What advice does Paul give to overcome it?

Bring It Home
(20 minutes, or as time allows)

Choose one of the following options.

Option 1
Listen to U2's song "Walk On" from the album *All That You Can't Leave Behind*. The Desert Fathers recommended commitment to stability (staying put and sticking to their spiritual disciplines; resisting the urge to flee) as the remedy for sloth. What situations do you find it difficult to "walk on" in? Does it have anything to do with "all that you can't leave behind"?

Option 2
As time permits, choose among the following questions and discuss them:

- How can an overly busy life actually be a sign of slothfulness? Do you ever get this sense from your own busy life? How do you fight excessive busyness—with its temptation to sloth—in your life? What works for you as ways of genuinely refreshing yourself and your relationship to God and others?

- Sloth can be defined as a lack of caring, thus putting off or ignoring what God wants us to do. Share some experiences of sloth in your life. What can you do about them?

Note: There is a difference between sinful sloth and clinical depression. The former is spiritual in nature, while the later has a physical basis. If you wonder which you may be experiencing, seek the advice of your pastor or trusted, spiritually mature friend.

- How can keeping up with spiritual disciples like prayer, Bible reading/study, silence and solitude help combat sloth? If these disciplines themselves seem useless or meaningless, should we take time off, hoping we will desire them again?

Option 3
Draw a cartoon that illustrates the common view of what sloth is (or read the children's book Revenge of the Sloths by Helen Lester). Then make a cartoon illustrating a slothful heart.

Pray It Through
(10 minutes)

Take time to suggest items to pray about together.

Make sure to suggest things that come to mind in your struggles with sloth, and then pray together as a group in whatever way you're accustomed.

As the prayer ends, have each group member pray through a line each of this prayer, and then read the last part in unsion.

O Lord God Almighty, who lives at once completely still and completely involved . . .

- Forgive me the slack-eyed nonresponse to something that should stir me to action, but barely elicits a yawn before the remote control switches to something more entertaining and less demanding.

- Forgive me for the passive acceptance without thought of somebody else's ideas and for the systematic way I avoid having to think deeply about anything.

- Forgive me the complacency with which I refuse to take responsibility, preferring instead to complain and talk about what someone else ought to do.

- Forgive me for letting love die when it demands action in order to live. Forgive me for not caring enough to mourn its death.

- Forgive me for the dainty shallow mediocrity of my following of Jesus, content to float along on the stream of someone else's spiritual passion—or not. . . .

Help me fall so deeply and passionately in love with you that I would do anything for the love of you. Help me to care about those things that you care about and to care as deeply as you do. Through Jesus Christ, the emblem of your passionate commitment to us and to the whole world. Amen.

(from http://www.vanguard.edu/uploadedFiles/Community/sfd/4_Sloth.pdf)

Live It Out

(Choose one of these suggestions for the coming week)

• Begin each day this week by singing or saying the words to Isaac Watts's famous hymn: "Were the whole realm of nature mine, that were a present far too small. Love so amazing, so divine, demands my soul, my life, my all."

• Pray a section of Psalm 119 each day (especially verses 25-32, targeting verse 28) at the "noonday" or in the midafternoon, whenever you find that your love for God and what he has called you to do and to be flagging.

Web Alert

Be sure to check out the participants' section for this session on www.GrowDisciples.org for interesting links and suggestions for readings and activities that will deepen your understanding of the sin of sloth.

Session 6
Greed

The Freedom of Generosity 1

"Then [Jesus] said to them, 'Watch out! Be on your guard against all kinds of greed; life does not consist in an abundance of possessions.' And he told them this parable: 'The ground of a certain rich man yielded an abundant harvest. He thought to himself, "What shall I do? I have no place to store my crops." 'Then he said, "This is what I'll do. I will tear down my barns and build bigger ones, and there I will store my surplus grain. And I'll say to myself, 'You have plenty of grain laid up for many years. Take life easy; eat, drink and be merry.'" 'But God said to him, "You fool! This very night your life will be demanded from you. Then who will get what you have prepared for yourself?"'"

—Luke 12:15-20

"Greed, ladies and gentlemen, greed—for lack of a better word— is good. Greed is right. Greed works." So goes Gordon Gecko's famous speech in the film *Wall Street*. American culture encourages it, and our patterns of consumption follow suit. Greed for gain seems benign, even necessary, for it is an American way of life—*our* way of life.

The spoof ad for greed in *Harper's* shows Santa with a child's letter in front him, which begins, "Dear Santa, I *want* . . ." Santa addresses the reader, "Do you remember all the things you told me you wanted as a child? Well, your list may have changed, but I bet it hasn't gotten any shorter."

The New Testament Greek calls this vice *pleonexia*—wanting more and more without limit or regard for others. In the Middle Ages, it was called avarice. We know it as just plain greed. It is the excessive desire for money and whatever money can buy. It is the dream of being able to supply all your needs and satisfy all your wants with what's in your wallet. It is the dream of having enough, or more than enough.

Scripture has nearly as much to say about greed as all the other vices combined. What it says is pretty harsh. The love of mammon is idolatry. The love

> **Word Alert**
>
> *Mammon* **is personified as the false god of riches and avarice.**

of money is the root of all evil. Judas betrayed his Lord for thirty pieces of silver. But we can't hear what Scripture preaches with jaded or complacent hearts.

Where do we begin thinking about greed? First we need to recognize that greed is primarily a heart problem. It is a matter of how attached we are to what we possess, and how much our desires are driven by wanting to possess more. We are greedy "on the inside" when we cling too tightly to money and stuff; when we're preoccupied with having and getting and securing it for ourselves. As with the other sins, however, excess and *dis*order have to be defined as deviations from *rightly* ordered desire. What does a rightly ordered attitude toward money and possessions look like? What is the virtue opposed to the sin of greed?

We usually call it generosity. I prefer the traditional term "liberality" because of its tie to "liberty." The opposite of greed's hunger for self-made security is freedom. Liberality is literally freedom from an attachment to money—the freedom to part with it, spend it, give it away. It should not to be confused with overspending it, wasting it, or parting with it foolishly. But holding our attachments to what we possess lightly, so that we can give them away when and where we ought without a painful separation: *that* is the freedom of generosity.

The widow who gives two copper coins to the temple treasury (Mark 12:41-44) is generous. Even in her poverty, she gives freely, trusting God to provide for tomorrow's need. Joseph of Arimathea is also generous. He donates his own newly cut tomb for Jesus' body. Whether our gift is large or small, whether we give 100 percent of our earnings or 10 percent of our savings, the sign of virtue is the cheerful willingness to part with money and what this reveals about the inner desires and attachments of the giver.

On the other hand, take Lot's choice of the finest, most fertile land in Genesis 13. He could have tried to work out a fairer deal with Abram, especially since Abram gave him first choice. But his greedy desire for the most and best for himself led him instead to choose Sodom as his new home, a choice that cost him his lifestyle and very nearly his life. Or consider the prodigal son demanding his share of the family fortune, wanting money so much he was willing to treat his father as if he were as good as dead. By contrast, listen to Jesus' parable about building bigger barns.

"It is enough for us to have only a little," says Aquinas, "so we should in general give away more than we keep." God gives some excess riches, he continues, "so that they might have the merit of good stewardship." What is money *for*? The greedy person says,

"For possessing." But the generous person knows that money's value is not in the having, but in the using, and using money requires parting with it.

How tightly are we holding onto money? How freely can we give it away?

Think It Over

1. What is the best example of generosity or freedom from attachment to money that you have experienced or seen?

2. What connection, if any, is there between having plenty of money and the ability to be generous?

In Other Words

"For what good would their prosperity do them if it did not provide them with the opportunity for good works?"

—Aristotle

Live It Out

Take note of the times today when you strongly desire something. It may come from an advertisement, or something you see that belongs to other people. What stimulates this desire? What itch will it scratch; what desire will it fulfill?

Mine! 2

"He has shown all you people what is good. And what does the LORD require of you? To act justly and to love mercy and to walk humbly with your God."

—Micah 6:8

Greed is primarily an "inside problem," a problem of excessive desire. The trouble is, because it is concerned so directly with money or possessions, it's hard to keep greed a private sin that harms only yourself. Greed shows up on the "outside" too.

When greed leads us to acquire and hoard money, even to the point of depriving others of their share, it becomes a justice issue. Greed's mantra—"Mine!"—eclipses our ability to see the needs of others. The desire for money can grow so relentless that we don't care who gets hurt as long as we get what we want.

In the words of St. Ambrose, "It is the hungry one's bread that you hoard, the naked one's cloak that you retain, the needy one's money that you withhold. Wherefore as many as you have wronged you might have aided." Picture Ebenezer Scrooge counting his coins while his clerk Bob Cratchit shivers in an under-heated room, working for a pittance that barely feeds his family. Or ponder the misery of King Midas, who turns his own daughter into gold. But can we picture the damage to others that *our* greed inflicts?

According to the Christian tradition, the sin of greed gives birth to "fraud, deceit, perjury, restlessness, violence, insensibility to mercy, and treachery." Aside from restlessness—the anxiety and constant craving that comes with always wanting more and never feeling secure enough with what we have—*all* of these have to do with getting money or keeping money unjustly. When greed makes its home in our heart, we grow blind to the needs of others. We become willing to deceive, defraud, and even destroy others in order to get what we want.

In 1 Kings 21, Ahab and Jezebel scheme and kill an innocent man to get their greedy hands on Naboth's vineyard. In the end, God sends the prophet Elijah to confront Ahab: "You have *sold yourself* to do evil in the eyes of the Lord" (1 Kings 21:20).

Is it surprising that greedy people will go to such lengths to get what they want? Greed is often described as a form of idolatry because it claims as our own what is really a gift held in trust. The greedy person forgets that he is a steward of creation, not its owner. He wants things to *belong* to him and to be under his control in the way that is only appropriate for God.

This is one way greed is rooted in pride, the root of the other sins. Greedy people take as their own what does not belong to them. We should not be astonished that they are willing to take from others by force or fraud as well.

When greed becomes an entrenched habit, we forget that money and possessions are for people, and for serving people. People are not instruments to be used to serve our acquisition of money. The film *Ocean's Eleven* depicts an ingenious theft of millions of dollars from Tony Benedict's casino, The Belagio. It's a revenge game for Danny Ocean, whose wife, Tess, has divorced him and gone to live with Tony. Danny and Tony are both thieves—although

Danny uses illegal means and Tony legal ones (running a casino). In a scene at the film's end, however, we see the true difference between them.

While Tess watches via security camera upstairs in the hotel, Danny asks Tony, "What if I told you I could get you your money back? Would you give up Tess? What would you say?" Tony replies coldly and matter-of-factly, "I would say yes." For Danny, however much he likes the money, Tess comes first. It's a turning point for Tess to see Tony exposed as the man truly sold out to greed.

Are you using your money to serve your love for people, or are you using other people to serve your love of money? It's a justice issue.

Think It Over

As the United States went through a recent economic downturn, the government decided to send every taxpayer a check for six hundred to twelve hundred dollars. The goal was to get people spending again, the worry that they might save it instead. To what extent is our economic system built on greed and covetousness? How does living in this culture affect us in our struggle with greed? How can the church or other Christians support us in that struggle?

In Other Words

"The trouble with being rich is that since you can solve with your checkbook virtually all practical problems that bedevil ordinary people, you are left in your leisure with nothing but the great human problems to contend with: how to be happy, how to love and be loved, how to find meaning and purpose in your life. In desperation the rich are continually tempted to believe that they can solve these problems too with their checkbooks, which is presumably what led Jesus to remark one day that for a rich man to get to Heaven is about as easy as for a Cadillac to get through a revolving door."

—Frederick Buechner, *Wishful Thinking*

Live It Out

Greed can make us blind to the needs of others. Identify a need in your neighborhood, church, or school. Then use your time, talents, or treasure to help meet that need.

No Fear 3

"Therefore I tell you, do not worry about your life, what you will eat or drink; or about your body, what you will wear. Is not life more important than food, and the body more important than clothes? Look at the birds of the air; they do not sow or reap or store away in barns, and yet your heavenly Father feeds them. Are you not much more valuable than they? Can any one of you by worrying add a single hour to your life? And why do you worry about clothes? See how the flowers of the field grow. They do not labor or spin. Yet I tell you that not even Solomon in all his splendor was dressed like one of these. If that is how God clothes the grass of the field, which is here today and tomorrow is thrown into the fire, will he not much more clothe you—you of little faith? So do not worry, saying, 'What shall we eat?' or 'What shall we drink?' or 'What shall we wear?' For the pagans run after all these things, and your heavenly Father knows that you need them. But seek first his kingdom and his righteousness, and all these things will be given to you as well. Therefore do not worry about tomorrow, for tomorrow will worry about itself. Each day has enough trouble of its own."

—Matthew 6:25-34

In his book *Following Jesus*, N. T. Wright says that we have a mistaken perception that God is a God of big and burdensome "Thou shalt nots." In fact, the most frequent command in the Bible, he writes, is a surprising one—"Don't be afraid."

He goes on, "The irony of this surprising command is that, though it's what we really all want to hear, we have as much difficulty obeying this command as any other. We all cherish fear so closely that we find we can't shed it even when we're told to do so."

How much of our hoarding and grasping for more stems from a deep-seated fear—a fear that we may not have even articulated for ourselves?

Aquinas says there are "two natural hindrances" to giving money away. The first is having earned it ourselves. When we have sweated for it, it feels like it is truly and ultimately our *own*. My brother and I used to fight over who got the privilege of putting our parent's money in the collection plate on Sunday. When it was *our* hard-earned money, however, it was a struggle to put in even 10 percent.

The second natural hindrance is having lived through a time of not having enough. For the generation who lived through the Depression, or for those who have known what it is like to *not* to have enough, it's difficult to ever feel like enough is enough. You can never be too careful; you can never have enough saved against misfortune and disaster, and you can never enjoy luxury now because there may be a shortfall later. One family found no less than $30,000 in cash stashed in an older woman's house when she passed away. Another couple retired in Florida but wouldn't spend the money to buy an air conditioner. The fear of want dies hard.

For many people, having enough money represents having security. No one would urge us to live imprudently or fail to save anything at all. But the "it's never enough" fears are always there. Greed can be a trust issue. The phrase on American money reads "In God we trust." Ironically, the money is what we often trust more.

God tried to teach the Israelites trust in the desert. He gave them manna every day—but only for that day. No hoarding, or it would spoil. No taking another's share or more than what was needed. Living on daily bread was a way to practice trusting God for future provision, a way to stave off the temptation to try to acquire what we need by ourselves.

Our trusty guide Evagrius of Pontus describes the way fear feeds our rationalizations to accumulate greedily: The demon of avarice "suggests a lengthy old age, inability to perform manual labor, famines that will come along, diseases that will arise, the bitter realities of poverty, and the shame there is in accepting goods from others to meet one's needs."

The ancient Christians associated two symptoms with an excessive attachment to one's possessions. The first is backward-looking—feeling too much sorrow over possessions we have lost or given away. Aquinas describes the dread some greedy people feel when they receive gifts because of the thought of having to give back in return. The second is forward-looking—a preoccupation with things desired but not yet acquired, or with fears of future needs that might possibly go unmet.

By contrast, the writer of Hebrews presents contentment and confidence as the roots of a life free from greed's excessive desires and attachments. "Keep your lives free from the love of money and be content with what you have, because God has said, 'Never will I leave you; never will I forsake you.' So we say with confidence, 'The Lord is my helper; I will not be afraid'" (Heb. 13:5-6).

Think It Over

1. How do we live out our trust in God to provide for what we need?

2. Do our spending and saving habits obey God's command not to live in fear?

In Other Words

"Do not be afraid, little flock, for your Father has been pleased to give you the kingdom. Sell your possessions and give to the poor. Provide purses for yourselves that will not wear out, a treasure in heaven that will never fail, where no thief comes near and no moth destroys. For where your treasure is, there your heart will be also."

—Luke 12:32-34

Live It Out

Make a list of your spending and saving for the last month. With several different color highlighters, mark what you spent and saved that was necessary. Analyze what is left—are you saving more than you need to? Did you have opportunities to give that you held back on? Why? What are you spending your "extra" on? Are these items that give you comfort or a feeling or protection against want?

The Love of Money 4

"Do not store up for yourselves treasures on earth, where moth and rust destroy, and where thieves break in and steal. But store up for yourselves treasures in heaven, where moth and rust do not destroy, and where thieves do not break in and steal. For where your treasure is, there your heart will be also. The eye is the lamp of the body. If your eyes are healthy, your whole body will be full of light. But if your eyes are unhealthy, your whole body will be full of darkness. If then the light within you is darkness, how great is that darkness! No one can serve two masters. Either you will hate the one and love the other, or you will be devoted to the one and despise the other. You cannot serve both God and Money."

—Matthew 6:19-24

Avarice, like the other sins, has its roots in pride. Pride is our usurping of God's place of power and control. Instead of turning our lives over to God and following his will for us, we try to run our lives our own way.

In a beautiful passage in the *Confessions*, Augustine describes the way our pride is a self-deceptive attempt to imitate God:

Pride imitates what is lofty; but you alone are God most high above all things. What does ambition seek but honor and glory? Yet you alone are worthy of honour and are glorious for eternity. The cruelty of powerful people aims to arouse fear. Who is to be feared but God alone? What can be seized or stolen from his power? . . . Idleness appears as desire for a quiet life; yet can rest be assured apart from the Lord? Luxury wants to be called abundance and satiety; but you are fullness and the inexhaustible treasure of incorruptible pleasure. Prodigality presents itself under the shadow of generosity; but you are the rich bestower of all good things. . . . So the soul fornicates (Ps. 72: 27) when it is turned away from you and seeks outside you the pure and clear intentions which are not to be found except by returning to you. In their perverted way all humanity imitates you.

How does our greed follow this pattern of prideful imitation of God? When it betrays a desire to control what we have and when we get it, a desire to provide what is needed for ourselves without having to depend on anyone else. It's a desire to be self-sufficient, without any need to trust God or acknowledge his ownership of what we have. Whatever form our greed takes, if it has this root, then our greed has turned idolatrous, as Jesus' warning in Matthew 6 implies.

"The love of money is a root of all kinds of evil," writes the apostle Paul (1 Tim. 6:10). Why is money a special danger? Is it because money gives us the means to satisfy any other desire we might have? Or is it because, more than anything else, it gives us the illusion that we can look to ourselves to satisfy all our desires? The love of money is a root of all kinds of evil because it is a powerful temptation to deny our dependence on God, to provide all the good things we need for ourselves, by ourselves.

Like the other sins, greed is rooted deeply in the heart and mind. To overcome its hold on us, we need to engage in regular practices that will ultimately change our hearts and make way for a new vision of the world. The point here is not to wallow in our guilt but to recognize the gravity of the problem and engage together in practices that will work against the grain of sin in our lives.

Several years ago, I gave a talk at the college where I teach called "Ten Things I Wished I Knew About Men Before I Married One." The talk was less about what I wished I knew about men than what I wished I knew about marriage. One of the lessons I shared with my students is that it's all too easy to think of marriage as a chance to build the perfect life and relationship together—all for ourselves. The mistake is to think of marriage as the key to my dream of personal happiness. What if marriage is instead a partnership that God creates and blesses so that the two of you can do something together for the kingdom that neither of you could do alone? Suddenly the purpose is turned outward, not inward.

Similarly, our attitude about money needs to be turned inside-out, lest it turn us inward toward a prideful, self-made, and ultimately selfish, conception of happiness. In that new vision, money is not for creating a perfect life for ourselves but to equip us for kingdom work that would not be possible without it.

Think It Over

How would you describe your relationship to your possessions? How might you want to change your habits and attitudes with respect to money in order to honor the kingdom vision described in this daily reading?

In Other Words

"And all the time the joke is that the word 'Mine' in its fully posses-sive sense cannot be uttered by a human being about anything. In the long run either [Satan] or [Christ] will say 'Mine' of each thing that exists, and specially of each man. They will find out in the end, never fear, to whom their time, their souls, and their bodies really belong—certainly not to them, whatever happens."

—C. S. Lewis, *Screwtape Letters*

Live It Out

Review your giving patterns for the past year. What causes or individuals do you support? Do some research and perhaps iden-tify a new charity that promotes God's kingdom cause to support with your time, treasure, and talents.

Simplicity 5

"The offering of the righteous enriches the altar, and its pleasing odor rises before the Most High. The sacrifice of the righteous is acceptable, and it will never be forgotten. Be generous when you worship the Lord, and do not stint the first fruits of your hands. With every gift show a cheerful face, and dedicate your tithe with gladness. Give to the Most High as he has given to you, and as generously as you can afford. For the Lord is the one who repays, and he will repay you sevenfold."

—Ecclesiasticus 35:8-13

Greed has a hold on most of us, and wresting free of its grip is something that we will likely have to work at for the rest of our lives. Rather than merely feeling guilty, however, we may take hold of specific practices that can—little by little—help break down fearful and prideful greed and build up trust and generosity.

Word Alert

The book of *Ecclesiasticus* (as distinct from Ecclesiastes) is found in a section of some Bibles called the Apocrapha or Deuterocanonical (secondary canon) books. These are writings from the Old Testament era that are not considered as inspired Scriptures by many churches, but are very helpful for Christians to read for personal spiritual growth.

I have found Richard Foster's *Freedom of Simplicity* to be a helpful guide in learning the inward and outward disciplines that can liberate us from a greedy mindset and a grasping lifestyle. One practice he suggests is this: When you decide you need something, wait a week (or two) to buy it. Pray about whether you in fact need the item, and ask God to provide it for you. "If it comes, bless God;" writes Foster, "if not, reevaluate your need for it; and if you still feel that you should have it, go ahead and purchase the item." He tells of a friend who needed a pair of gloves and, even though he never spoke this need aloud, someone gave him a pair a few days later. When this happens, suggests Foster, we can give away the money we *would* have spent on the item to avoid using God's provision for our own gain.

In a *Christianity Today* article called "The Devil Takes VISA," Rodney Clapp suggests several ways of opting out of a "consumer lifestyle"—one that feeds our desires to accumulate more and leaves our aspirations to affluence unchecked.

We can take small steps toward taking a Sabbath rest from feeding our greed. For instance, by choosing recreation that doesn't cost money—like preparing food for a picnic or having a game night with friends or family. Or by decreasing our exposure to advertising by avoiding the mall for a month, or recycling catalogs that come in the mail without opening them, or watching a carefully chosen movie each week with others instead of spending weeknights in front of the TV.

Both Clapp and Foster also suggest deliberately capping our spending. They suggest budgeting in order to know what we're spending money on and increasing our tithe as ways to include regular checks on greed in our life.

So go for it! Try living at your current level of spending or income for a year rather than ramping up as you get more. Give the extra away. Give gifts regularly and on unexpected occasions—in fact, try giving some sort of undeserved gift (even your time or assistance) every day. We may even find that generous giving and limiting our spending frees us from our obsession with acquiring things and opens us to other activities.

Once again we need to remind ourselves that the goal of engaging in these disciplines is to re-form our hearts inwardly, and to do so without legalism. We persevere in these holy habits not to conform to a rigid behavioral code but to free our hearts for love.

At first these habits may be difficult to practice. But in the end, they will yield a breath of fresh air, and we will find relief from the burden of always thinking about how we will get the next thing for ourselves. At the same time, we'll experience the joy and peace of simplicity in our lives.

Think It Over

Richard Foster talks about practicing simplicity in our use of time and money and emotional investments. Can you think of a time when your ability to say no to something (a purchase, possession, commitment, or person) helped you feel the freedom of simplicity? What is the biggest obstacle to making that freedom part of your life?

In Other Words

"The sea does not reward those who are too anxious, too greedy, or too impatient. One should lie empty, open, choiceless as a beach waiting for a gift from the sea."

—Anne Morrow Lindbergh, *Gift from the Sea*

Live It Out

Make a list of the ways you might simplify your life and make it more joyful and satisfying at the same time.

Greed

Discussion Guide

Greed, or avarice as it is also known, is a familiar vice. It is defined as excessive love and attachment to money (or whatever money can buy).

Scripture has numerous and harsh warnings about greed, and many familiar stories of those ruined or nearly ruined by it. But what is at the heart of this sin, and how can we break its hold on us?

Our desire for more and more money, and our desire to hold on too tightly to what we have, are fed primarily by two roots—fear and pride. We seek to provide and hoard for ourselves because we are afraid of not having enough, afraid to trust God to provide for us, and afraid to depend on anyone else. We also pridefully seek to become self-sufficient through wealth so that we don't need to look to God for what we need or acknowledge his ownership of all that we possess.

Greed can and does hurt others, but it also does internal damage. The primary ways to overcome greed are to loosen our grip on what we have and to practice giving it away. Good stewardship is a great start—for we need to relearn that what we have is ours to steward well, not to own— but the full freedom of generosity is the goal.

For Starters

(10 minutes)

Stories of greed are common enough and make good headlines. But how about examples of generosity? Mention one example of generosity in the news that really impressed you. Or tell about an act of generosity that someone extended to you or that you witnessed or heard about.

Or, invite group members to share one insight from the daily devotions or the "Living it Out" exercises from last week that was meaningful for them. Don't discuss it now, just mention it.

Let's Focus

(5 minutes)

Review the introduction to this session, and then have someone read this focus statement aloud:

Scripture has many warnings about greed because it can so easily lead us to substitute our own provisions for God's provision. When this happens, money becomes an idol and other people become instruments of our need for more. Rather than using money to serve God and our love for others, we use God and others to serve our love for money.

Word Search

(20 minutes)

Discuss the following Scripture passages (or, if you're running short on time, choose the ones the group wants to discuss):

* 1 Kings 21:1-19
  What motivates Ahab's greed? Jezebel's action?

  Why do you think greed often infects the rich and powerful even more than the poor and powerless (where we might expect it)?

* Luke 12:13-21
  What does greed do to the rich man in Jesus' parable?

  What does it mean to be "rich toward God"?

  What's the main lesson about the futility of greed in this story?

  Right away Jesus seems to issue a special warning regarding greed. Why?

- Colossians 3:5
  Paul says that greed is the same thing as idolatry (worshiping a false god). Why is this true of greed perhaps more than other sins? (see also Matt. 6:24).

Bring It Home
(20 minutes, or as time allows)
Choose one of the following options.

Option 1
Divide into two groups and **have a contest to see which group can list the most greed-inspired TV shows/films/popular songs.** Then rank which ones are your favorites. Discuss together why you think we find these sorts of things entertaining?

Option 2
As time permits, choose among the following questions and discuss them:

- It's hard to fight greed in our culture. Name all the things in culture you can think of (books, music, movies) that promote and glorify greed. How do you fight against that pervasive influence?

- Giving our money away is one very effective way to combat greed. But how do we know how much to give away? Is the tithe (10 percent) an effective guide, in your experience? Or is it better to simply "give as the Lord has blessed us?" Since generosity or giving is a spiritual discipline, what might the *discipline* involve?

- In what areas of your life do you most easily get hooked by greed? See if there are any patterns in your group. Brainstorm ways to combat greed in these areas.

Option 3

Get a DVD of the film *Jerry Maguire* and **watch the "Show Me the Money" scene** together. (We don't recommend watching the rest of the film because it contains some inappropriate material.) How do Ron and Jerry teach other about the value of money and the value of people in this film? How does Ron's "show me the money" attitude change by the end of the film? How does Jerry learn about contentment from Ron?

Pray It Through

(10 minutes)

Take time to suggest items to pray about together.

As you have shared some of your struggles with greed, pray for each other, asking God for forgiveness, wisdom, and generosity.

Perhaps the group would like to sing at the close of the prayer. Sing or say the words to "In the Lord I'll Be Ever Thankful" (*Sing! A New Creation*, 220) quietly several times to close your prayer.

Live It Out

(Today, or every day this week)

Write out the words of Philippians 4:11-14, 19 and read it several times during the day. Take note of feelings of discontent, and give them to God in trust and prayer.

> (Web Alert)
>
> **Be sure to check out the partici-pants' section for this session on www.GrowDisciples.org for inter-esting links and suggestions for readings and activities that will deepen your understanding of the sin of greed.**

Session 7
Lust

Mixed Messages 1

"Place me like a seal over your heart,
like a seal on your arm;
for love is as strong as death,
its jealousy unyielding as the grave.
It burns like blazing fire,
like a mighty flame.

Many waters cannot quench love;
rivers cannot sweep it away.
If one were to give
all the wealth of one's house for love,
it would be utterly scorned."
—Song of Songs 8:6-7

It is very easy to find distortions of sexuality all around us, including within the church. You can't walk through the checkout lane in the grocery store, drive past billboards, or watch a half-hour of television without being exposed to perversions of sexuality that portray the world as a meat market for sins of the flesh. On the other hand, you can't listen to Christian radio and hear a love song addressed to anyone but Jesus, as if loving another flesh-and-blood human being might be too suspect to sing about in a Christian song.

Sex is the god our culture worships as the key to happiness; at the same time, it's the impetus for casual weekend hook-ups, no strings attached. Sex is often a taboo subject in churches, other than an occasional "purity weekend" run by the youth pastor, but at the same time, marriage and children are venerated to the point of making singles feel excluded. In our culture, the worst possible thing that could befall you is becoming a 40-year-old virgin; in our churches, the worst possible thing that could befall you is becoming pregnant out of wedlock. Talk about mixed messages!

Why is sex such a big deal? Why can't we talk about it? Why can't we stop talking about it? How can we ever find a sane word about lust in a church and a culture dominated by taboos and those who flaunt them?

> **Word Alert**
>
> *Purity weekends* are **retreats for both teens and adults held in some churches focusing on making a commitment to sexual purity.**

It's true that Christians have a lot of bad things to say about lust—and probably more bad things to say about lust than about greed, sexism, abuse, and racism combined. To people outside the church and inside too, this sin sometimes seems to get more attention than it deserves. Even Paul's lists of great sins in his epistles have more warnings about idolatry, anger, and greed than lust. So what gives?

Let's start with a definition: Sex is an act of intimacy that bonds two people into one flesh. It's for bonding people together in relationships of love. In addition, sex is a reproductive act that brings new human life into being. Since sex is about love and life, Christians have good reason to get upset about lust and sexual sins. It's not a trivial thing to mess up on love or life, or both.

The key is to focus on the love- and life-giving character of sex, not its distortions. In Scripture we find a testimony to the beauty and power of the gift of sexuality, the goodness of our bodies, and the blessings of life and love that flow to God's people through sex, not in spite of it. Sex deserves our healthy respect, not our fear and condemnation.

Think It Over

When was the last time you heard a message about sex that did not either warn of its dangers or exaggerate its recreational pleasures? Can you think of an example of a beautiful marriage (or life of singleness) that inspires you?

In Other Words

"Contrary to Mrs. Grundy, sex is not a sin. Contrary to Hugh Hefner, it's not salvation either. Like nitroglycerin, it can be used either to blow up bridges or heal hearts."

—Frederick Buechner, *Wishful Thinking*

Live It Out

Think about what you can do this week (in your language, your storytelling, your reading, your encouragement to others, your witness, your treatment of your spouse or your friends, your conversations with children) to promote the beauty of rightly-ordered sexuality and sexual activity this week. Put your ideas into practice.

Love Versus Lust 2

"Do not love the world or anything in the world. If you love the world, love for the Father is not in you. For everything in the world—the cravings of sinful people, the lust of their eyes and their boasting about what they have and do—comes not from the Father but from the world. The world and its desires pass away, but whoever does the will of God lives forever."

—1 John 2:15-17

The seven deadly sins achieve their status on the list by being happiness-imitators. Each involves pursuing good things in an excessive or disordered way. As part of our attempt to create happiness for ourselves, we use (or more accurately, misuse) them as essential props. Happiness is . . . money, power and control, esteem and approval, and *pleasure*.

Lust and gluttony are the sins of the flesh, vices born of our craving for physical pleasure. Lust is defined as an excessive desire for self-centered sexual pleasure. While pleasure, and sexual pleasure, are good things, they can be pursued rightly or wrongly. To define lust as a sin, then, does not condemn sexual pleasure as such.

As fire is warm and pleasurable when contained in a fireplace, so sexual desire yields pleasure and good things when expressed within appropriate boundaries. Lust can go wrong in two main ways: when sexual desire is directed at the wrong object, or when its manner of expression is excessive.

Both of these ways reflect sexual desire going "out of bounds." When sexual desire is directed at someone with whom you ought not have sex or sexual intimacy—anyone other than a spouse—it is out of bounds. Anyone can feel sexual urges, and plenty of times, these may arise unintentionally. But are they indulged, cultivated, consented to, fantasized about, and turned into action? The desire, when it is backed by the will and becomes habitual, is a sin— whether or not it is ever acted upon. Lust is a way of looking at the world through the eyes of your own pleasure. It begins in the mind and feeds on fantasy.

Even when sexual desire has the right object, it can still fall into lust through excess. Sexual desire is excessive when it becomes a demand for gratification that does not respect another, including your spouse. Aquinas is not known for the respectful ways he treats women and their full humanity. But in his treatise on lust, he says that misusing your spouse for your own selfish pleasure is a breach of the marriage covenant and can be as grave a sin as adultery.

Often the two forms of lust go together: we feel free to let our desire run unchecked because we see others as our personal play- ground, whether that other is a spouse or a casual acquaintance.

Finally, lust need not be consummated in sex to be lust. Lust is a problem with the heart above your belt before it is a problem below it.

Probably the best way to see what's gone wrong with lust is to compare it with the way things ought to be between people.

- Love is about the giving and receiving of gifts; lust is about taking.

- Love is self-giving; lust is selfish.
- Love is about relationships with others; lust uses others for physical gratification.
- Love allows us to become more fully human; lust dehumanizes us and others.
- Love respects and fosters life; lust chokes our spiritual life and harms others.
- Love honors and protects what is sacred; lust keeps nothing out of the public eye.
- Love honors the way our bodies are made; lust uses bodies as an instrument of pleasure.
- Love is content; lust always craves more.

The tricky thing about pleasure, as the ancient Greek philosophers noted already two millennia ago, is that it always tracks a certain sort of activity. The pleasure of reading a good book is not the same as the pleasure of snowboarding. The pleasure of reading a good mystery novel is not the same as the pleasure of reading a well-written tragedy. The pleasure of reading to myself is not the same as the pleasure of reading to my children.

This is true of sexual pleasure too. The pleasure of making love to a spouse in a secure, loving marriage is not the same as the pleasure of masturbating or making it all the way with a hot date. The pleasure of conquest is not the same as the pleasure of relief, which is not the same as the pleasure of being welcomed in love, body and soul. (Sexual activity can also be robbed of pleasure by fear or woundedness or disrespect, but this is another sort of problem.)

Lustful sex cannot deliver the pleasure that loving sex can, and its pleasures cannot stand the test of time. Lustful pleasure has a desperate, "I want it, I have to have it" edge. Lust says "me." Love says "we."

Think It Over

Our culture is saturated with messages of distorted sexuality. What are some ways we can surround ourselves with examples of healthy sexuality? Can you think of examples in books, movies, television?

In Other Words

"At its roots, the hunger for food is the hunger for survival. At its roots the hunger to know a person sexually is the hunger to know and be known by that person humanly. Food without nourishment doesn't fill the bill for long, and neither does sex without humanness."

—Frederick Buechner, *Wishful Thinking*

Live It Out

Read through the beautiful, exuberant poetry of the Song of Songs. Notice how the lovers receive the gift of their beloved with gratitude and celebration. It's the opposite of the me-centered lust so often portrayed in our culture.

Collateral Damage 3

"It is God's will that you should be sanctified: that you should avoid sexual immorality; that each of you should learn to control your own body in a way that is holy and honorable, not in passionate lust like the pagans, who do not know God; and that in this matter no one should wrong or take advantage of a brother or sister. The Lord will punish all those who commit such sins, as we told you and warned you before. For God did not call us to be impure, but to live a holy life."

—1 Thessalonians 4:3-7

One reason lust is such a powerful temptation to sin is its promise of pleasure, fun, and happiness. Our culture often treats sex as a harmless, recreational activity. But is it really?

Second Samuel 11 tells the famous story of David's adultery with Bathsheba and all the hurt that follows. The soldier Uriah is murdered by the king he served; his loyalty to his wife, king, and comrades is betrayed. Bathsheba loses her husband (when David arranges for his murder), and she and David lose their baby. The generals and messengers in the army are the victim of lies and can no longer trust their leader; and the whole community sees King David immersed in shame and disgrace.

By God's grace, shame and disgrace were not the last word for David. The collateral damage of David's lust didn't go away, but his relationship with God was restored when he confessed his sin after being confronted by the prophet Nathan. Psalm 51 is widely seen as the expression of David's repentance.

Adultery is a lie, and lies need to be covered up. Any kind of sex outside out of the bounds God created, for that matter, is a lie. Sex is a way of saying "I give myself to you" and "I receive your gift of yourself to me." So sex that takes instead of gives is a lie. And who isn't hurt when they are lied to?

Love and good sex require integrity, faithfulness, trust, and promise-keeping. Lust breaks these essential social bonds down, and breaks down human relationships with it. As the story of David and Bathsheba shows, lust does damage to others, often indirectly impacting those who aren't directly involved.

Contemporary examples of this damage abound. A sex offender who moves into a neighborhood feels like a threat to the whole community. Teens having sex early put pressure on their peers and hurt their future marriage partner. Explicit magazines, billboards, and TV programs expose children to inappropriate sexual content. Sexual abuse and affairs rip families and churches apart. We should note too that the statistics of this sort of damage are no different inside the church than outside it. At heart, lust ruins our ability to trust each other and love each other.

But there are less sensational cases of damage, too—the social "smoke damage" from the fires of lust that we can't even always put our finger on. We may find ourselves plagued by a nagging feeling that things don't feel right or comfortable. A recent study at a Christian college showed that at least 70 percent of the males on campus had viewed hard-core pornography on the Internet. You may stop looking at porn (although you are more likely to join the ranks of the addicted majority), but everyone knows the power of an image and the way it stays with you. How does it change a classroom atmosphere when over half of the men looking back at their female professor may have just come off a late night of viewing porn? How does it change your inclination to go on a date with one of them, or to know your daughter will do so? How does it change male-female relations at work or at church or at home when the majority of men have used porn for recreation? How does it change the ability of those 70 percent to love and make love to their own future wives? Lust's smoke poisons the air we need to breathe, even if we don't get burned by the flames.

Lust is addictive—a huge high that easily becomes a habit. Although some may find it hard to believe that lust is a real problem ("What's so bad about peeking at the Playmate of the month?"), there's no denying that lust is a habit, and habits have the power to form or deform us. When we become deformed enough, we hardly look human anymore, nor can we function well in human relationships.

As Frederick Buechner observes in his book *Wishful Thinking*, "Who is to say who gets hurt and who doesn't get hurt, and how? Maybe the injuries are all internal. Maybe it will be years before the X-rays show up anything. Maybe the only person who gets hurt is you."

Think It Over

Compare the way we seek pleasure and self-gratification in food to the way we seek it in sex. How are the two similar? How are they different? Does either one have greater "collateral damage"? Why?

In Other Words

"Everyone knows that people treat rental cars like crap. Why? Because it's not theirs. It doesn't belong to them. So they'll run over anything. Curbs. Road trash. Small circus ponies. Anything. . . . Sex without marriage is like a rental car. People will use you. Drive you around. And then, it's no problem to get rid of you. Why? 'Cause there's no commitment. No ownership."

—Justin Lookadoo, *The Dirt on Sex*

Live It Out

Listen to a contemporary song or television show that portrays lust (for example, John Mayer's "Your Body Is a Wonderland" or the episode from *The Office* called "A Benihana Christmas" (season 3, 2006). Consider how lust is portrayed, and how pervasive these examples are. What steps can you take to limit the damage of lust in your life?

Sticky Tape 4

"The body, however, is not meant for sexual immorality but for the Lord, and the Lord for the body. By his power God raised the Lord from the dead, and he will raise us also. Do you not know that your bodies are members of Christ himself? Shall I then take the members of Christ and unite them with a prostitute? Never! Do you not know that he who unites himself with a prostitute is one with her in body? For it is said, 'The two will become one flesh.' But whoever is united with the Lord is one with him in spirit. Flee from sexual immorality. All other sins people commit are outside their bodies, but those who sin sexually sin against their own bodies. Do you not know that your bodies are temples of the Holy Spirit, who is in you, whom you have received from God? You are not your own; you were bought at a price. Therefore honor God with your bodies."

—1 Corinthians 6:13b-20

Sometimes we are tempted to make our spiritual lives too spiritual. To grow spiritually, we need to pray more often, worship more fervently, memorize more Scripture. It's true; we do need to do these things. But what if to grow spiritually, we also needed to treat our bodies better? And the bodies of others too?

Paul insists in this passage that we can't split ourselves in two—the "inner me" and its "outer case," the body. The truth is, you can't do things with your body that don't affect your heart and mind, and you can't do things with your heart and mind that don't affect your body.

Look at the way anxiety and grief affect us physically: we lose our appetite, we can't sleep, our blood pressure rises, we die sooner. Look at the way our bodies affect our hearts and minds: when we don't get enough sleep, we feel depressed and more easily irritated; after we exercise, we feel more self-respect and have a brighter outlook on the world. Part of the reason for the Sabbath is that God knew that *both* our minds and our bodies needed to rest and be refreshed periodically. The physical rhythms of the day and week and the church year are essential to making room for God in our hearts.

What you do with your body affects your heart. Human beings were created as embodied creatures, and that is how we will be resurrected. So Paul says whomever you unite your body with becomes part of you. This is the truth of being human—an embodied, sexual being. Respecting yourself and respecting God requires respecting bodies—yours and your neighbor's.

John Mayer wrote a song a few years ago called "Your Body Is a Wonderland." The song portrayed his lover's body as a playground or amusement park—a place to have fun and explore for a while and then, when the time is up, to leave behind, along with the trash on the ground and the bits of cotton candy stuck to the sweaty, vinyl seats. What if we thought of our own bodies as holy temples instead? Would you leave bits of trash and cotton candy on the floor of a cathedral? Would you host a carnival with cheap thrills in the church sanctuary?

Yesterday we focused on the way disordered sexual desire harms others. Today we look at the way it harms us. Studies have shown that illicit sexual activity leads to greatly increased rates of depression, low self-esteem, and suicide (along with other self-destructive behaviors) in teens. There is no self-loathing like the feelings of a pornography addict. In his book *The Dirt on Sex*, Justin Lookadoo named these results "emotional STDs." Even if you don't get gonorrhea or genital warts, you haven't escaped without damage.

You can't take the soul out of sex and make it pure bodily recreation, because you *are* your body. Lust can deliver instant pleasure. Why else would anyone go back for more? But it also delivers disrespect—of ourselves and others. Lust erodes our ability to love ourselves the morning after, even if we don't notice it at first. Jesus commands us to love our neighbors *as ourselves*. We can't respect our neighbor and his or her body if we can't respect ourselves and our own bodies. Those who cannot love themselves and treat themselves with respect are impaired in their ability to love others and relate to them in an appropriate sexual way. The habit of pursuing lustful pleasure as a cheap and easy happiness substitute delivers self-made unhappiness instead.

My students and I sometimes engage in an exercise that illustrates the effects of lust and its accompanying behavior on us. It counters the common myth that whatever consenting adults do won't hurt anyone, least of all themselves. Everyone gets a twelve-inch strip of duct tape and five minutes to stick to as many others and other objects as they can. Each person's tape starts clean and powerfully sticky. By the end of the five minutes, however, the strips of tape are crinkled, torn, and shredded. Bits of others' tape is permanently stuck to it, and it has lost its stickiness. The students' comments at the end of the exercise are instructive: "Part of so-and-so is still stuck to me and I can't get that piece off." "I stuck to so many things that I can't stick to anything anymore."

One time, a student and I stuck our pieces of tape carefully together from end to end. Although we spent the rest of the time trying, we could not get them apart at all. What a picture of the "one flesh" truth about sex! Do you believe it?

Think It Over

1. What can you do to show respect for others and their bodies? How can your ordinary, daily gestures, jokes, language, and touch be a witness to the respect due to other human beings?

2. How can touching a person make a personal connection? How can touch be used to express and serve love rather than lust?

In Other Words

"Unclench your fists
Hold out your hands.
Take mine.
Let us hold each other.
Thus is his Glory
Manifest."

—Madeleine L'Engle, "Epiphany," *The Ordering of Love*

Live It Out

This week, think of a specific way to "honor God with your body"—and do so.

Chastity 5

"Daughters of Jerusalem, I charge you:
Do not arouse or awaken love
until it so desires."

—Song of Songs 8:4

The main trouble with lust is that we can be completely convinced that lust ruins love between human beings and still feel unable to resist it. Americans are more educated about nutrition than any other nation in the world, and we are also the unhealthiest eaters with the most prevalent food-induced diseases. So you can preach all you want about how lust is disordered and all the rest, just like you can preach all you want about high fiber and modest portion sizes. But when the beach fills with bikinis and the dessert plate is offered, there it is. Education has not exorcised the demon.

Overcoming lust, like overcoming gluttony, requires daily discipline and accountability. These sins typically cause shame, and shame causes us to want to hide. When we are hiding we cannot get help, nor can we help ourselves. If lust is our problem, we need help getting out of its grip, and for that we need other people.

Statistics show that 90 percent of dieters fail to keep off lost weight. This is why the diet industry makes billions a year. Sheer individual willpower works just about as well on lust. Lust, like gluttony, cannot remain private.

That means chastity must be a corporate, community effort. The church cannot remain silent and pretend the problem doesn't exist. And chastity must be a positive, proactive program, not a narrow lust-avoidance program.

To curb lust, we need to structure our lives in ways that avoid isolation and allow us to cultivate healthy friendships with members of both sexes. If you sit in front of a computer all day in your office and temptation is just a breath away, make sure your computer screen is visible to anyone looking into your office, and take regular breaks to eat lunch with coworkers. Know when you are most vulnerable, and schedule alternative events or call a friend during those times. Get software that e-mails all the websites you visit to an accountability partner, and install an Internet filter. Or get rid of the computer at home. Find someone who is willing to ask how you are doing and check up on you regularly.

Dress modestly and hang out with others who do. Turn every comment on someone's appearance into an opportunity to compliment something they did or said instead. Keep your language, jokes, and stories clean. Refuse to use any sexual slang. Regularly read Scripture to remind yourself that God loves you and wants the most beautiful and best for you. Chastity—the virtue of a healthy appreciation for sexual desire, expressed in God-honoring ways—is a lifestyle, not a last-minute "no" in the face of temptation.

Lust begins in the imagination and centers on fantasy, not reality. So choose to fill your eyes and mind and heart with things of real beauty and worth. "Finally, brothers and sisters, whatever is true, whatever is noble, whatever is right, whatever is pure, whatever is lovely, whatever is admirable—if anything is excellent or praiseworthy—think about such things (Phil. 4:8). Nature abhors a vacuum. Your mind *will* be full—but of what?

In the end, probably the most effective advice on how to counter lust is not a list of "don'ts." It's this: *have good friends.* Make friendships your focus; cultivate good relationships with others. Learn how to care for them and to give and receive physical affection from them in appropriate ways. Respect them and trust them and rely on them. The more you keep your life deeply rooted in love for others, the less you are likely to be moved by temptations to substitute lust for love, or to look for a quick fix from lust to get you through a difficult or lonely time. The antidote to lust is to build a relationship with God and others that feeds your need for love, so you aren't tempted to swap it for something less fulfilling.

One of the marks of a life taken captive by lust is losing our ability to recognize and appreciate the beauty of real goods—the goods of sex, love, other women and men. As one blogger on the website xxxchurch.com put it, "As a struggling porn addict myself, I know what the producer said about porn getting more and more brutal on the women is true, and it will only get worse. [There's] something about human nature that gets desensitized to the ordinary. So I will continue to pray for this mission."

It is a mark of a life taken captive to love that lustful pleasures look less and less appealing, the way the glamour and glitz of a Hollywood lifestyle fails to appeal to those who know the contentment and comfort of a real home.

Think It Over

1. How would you recommend practicing chastity to a teenager today? Is it advice you could have followed yourself? Why or why not?

2. What would it look like to walk beside that teen, or your own friends and colleagues, as we practice chastity together? What sort of support would help *you*?

In Other Words

"What we call 'being in love' is a glorious state, and, in several ways, good for us. It helps to make us generous and courageous, it opens our eyes not only to the beauty of the beloved but to all beauty, and it subordinates . . . our merely animal sexuality; in that sense, love is the great conqueror of lust."

—C. S. Lewis, *Mere Christianity*

Live It Out

Choose one or two of the strategies mentioned in today's reading for structuring your life in ways that avoid isolation and allow you to develop good relationships. Make a habit of them!

Lust
Discussion Guide

The church has a bad reputation for making sex seem sinful and lust the worst possible sin. While most lust begins with curiosity about some forbidden or excessive passion, rather than a deliberate wish to sin or harm another, the connection of sex to life and love make the consequences of this disordered desire serious.

It is important to remember and emphasize that God created human sexuality good and powerful and beautiful. We are to respect sex, not demonize it, or the body, or the opposite sex. On the other hand, given how powerfully binding and addictive sexual desire can be, it's important to take seriously our need for both accountability and chastity (the virtue of respecting our sexuality and keeping our desires for it rightly ordered in love).

Our culture both overemphasizes and trivializes sex. It tells us that sex has the power to make us happy, and at the same time that it is only casual recreation. Whether we recognize it or not, we are shaped by these attitudes. The church can and should tell counter-stories that celebrate the greatness and beauty of genuine love relationships and the power and pleasure of sex within loving marriages. We also need to warn each other of the hurt to everyone that comes from lust's empty and self-centered search for sexual gratification.

For Starters
(10 minutes)

Divide into small groups of two or three persons each. Each group should have a large sheet of newsprint and a marker. The groups have three minutes to list all the myths about sex/sexuality that they can think of (make sure someone keeps track of time). When the three minutes are up, display the lists and review and compare together. Talk about where these myths come from and how widely they are accepted.

Or invite group members to share one insight from the daily devotions or the "Living It Out" suggestion from last week that was meaningful for them. Don't discuss it now, just mention it.

Let's Focus
(5 minutes)

Review the introduction to this session, and then have someone read this focus statement aloud:

Lust is disordered sexual desire—disordered because it transgresses the boundaries God has set for good sex and because it reduces sexual desire to selfishness. Sexual desire and the sexual acts that express it appropriately are meant to serve life and be a sign of self-giving love. Lust, on the other hand, generates self-hatred and disrespect for others. It can promise and deliver sexual pleasure long enough to get us hooked, which gives it great power. But in the end, the habit of lust ruins our ability to love and be loved. It warps our ability to see and appreciate the goodness and beauty in sex that God himself has created.

Word Search
(20 minutes)

Discuss the following Scripture passage (or choose ones the group wants to discuss):

- 2 Samuel 11
  Read the familiar story of David and Bathsheba from 2 Samuel 11 and then discuss the questions below (also see day 3 of the daily readings for the author's comments on this passage).

David was a rich and powerful king, loved by the Lord and the people. How do you explain his wanting and taking Bathsheba?

What typical elements of lust do you see here?

What commandments did David ultimately break because of his lust? Review the harmful effects of his adultery on himself and on all the others in the story.

This story happened thousands of years ago yet it's strikingly contemporary and powerfully instructive. What can we—who live in a culture whose god is sex—take to heart from this ancient story?

Bring It Home
(20 minutes, or as time allows)

Choose one of the following options.

Option 1

Kids today—as never before—are bombarded with the wrong images of sex from TV, movies, the Internet, rock stars, and peers. **Share some of your struggles with teaching your children or other children you love the difference between love and lust.** Can you think of any positive images of sex in our culture?

Option 2

As time permits, choose among the following questions and discuss them:

- Explain: "Lust is a problem with the heart above your belt before it is a problem with the heat below it" (from day 2).

- Do men and women experience lust differently? Discuss what you think are the differences, and the corresponding temptations for each gender.

- What are the best strategies or practices you have found to combat the temptation to lust, especially living in a sex-saturated culture as we do?

Option 3

Since we live in a sex-saturated culture think of yourself as a team facing a big game. **Analyze the offense . . . the media, the Internet, and all the other purveyors of cheap sex. Strategize your defense in response to these "plays."** Maybe you'll want to use labeled Xs and Os on a board or sheet of newsprint.

Pray It Through

(10 minutes)

Take time to suggest items to pray about together.

As individuals, think back over the seven deadly sins rooted in pride we've studied in this course: vainglory, envy, wrath, gluttony, sloth, greed, lust. Which of these do you struggle with most? Think quietly about this for a few moment.

Then have someone read 2 Peter 1:3-8:

"His divine power has given us everything we need for a godly life through our knowledge of him who called us by his own glory and good-ness. Through these he has given us his very great and precious promises, so that through them you may participate in the divine nature, having es-caped the corruption in the world caused by evil desires. For this very rea-son, make every effort to add to your faith goodness; and to goodness, knowledge; and to knowledge, self-control; and to self-control, persever-ance; and to perseverance, godliness; and to godliness, mutual affection; and to mutual affection, love. For if you possess these qualities in increas-ing measure, they will keep you from being ineffective and unproductive in your knowledge of our Lord Jesus Christ."

Thank God that he has given you "everything we need for a godly life," enumerating these things from the passage and as they come to mind.

Ask God specifically for the virtues enumerated in this passage.

then take time to ask God's forgiveness and for the presence of the Holy Spirit to help you overcome.

Conclude by saying the prayer (in unison) with which we began this course:

"Direct us, O Lord, in all our doings, with your most gracious favor, and further us with your continual help; that in all our works begun, continued, and ended in you, we may glorify your holy name, and finally, by your mercy, obtain everlasting life, through Jesus Christ our Lord, Amen." (from *The Book of Common Prayer*)

Live It Out

We overcome sin by understanding how it operates, receiving God's grace when we fail, and instilling practices or disciplines in our lives to strengthen us spiritually. There are many spiritual disciplines. Commit yourself to exploring them. Here are some helpful resources:

- *The Spirit of the Disciplines,* Dallas Willard
- *Celebration of Discipline*, Richard Foster.
- *The Spiritual Disciplines Handbook*, Adele Ahlberg Calhoun

(Web Alert)

Also make sure to visit our website, www.GrowDisciples.org, for lots more to explore on the spiritual disciplines and the seven deadly sins.